Introduction

It's true. With a little study and practice, anyone can play piano—and this proven piano program will give you the chance to play a variety of popular styles—including rock, pop, blues, jazz, ragtime, and classical music. The easy, step-by-step method will guide you through all the basics of piano performance and technique. You'll strengthen and develop these important playing skills in exciting performance sessions when you play the popular hits of Elvis Presley, the Beach Boys, Cream, the Animals—as well as memorable tunes recorded by James Taylor, Judy Collins, Bing Crosby, Ella Fitzgerald, Sam Cooke, Ritchie Valens, and Los Lobos. Also included are the all-time favorite songs that every pianist needs to know for performing at special occasions and parties—such as "The Entertainer," "For He's a Jolly Good Fellow," "The Wedding March," "Auld Lang Syne," "Pomp and Circumstance," "Jingle Bells," and "Silent Night."

This comprehensive piano method is easy and fun—and does not rely on tricks and shortcuts that only work for certain songs in certain keys. On the contrary, you can learn to sightread a variety of piano music in different keys—and develop all the skills you need to play hundreds of new songs on your own after you finish the program.

Whether you intend to be a professional pianist or songwriter, or simply wish to play for your community, family, and friends—this book is for you. So, get ready to learn the basics of piano as you play the world's most popular songs.

Your Piano

This book is designed to be used with any keyboard instrument—ranging from a medium-sized electric piano to a concert grand. Whether you own, rent, or use a friend's piano, you'll soon develop a close relationship with all piano keyboards that will last a lifetime.

If you are using an electronic keyboard, it should have at least twenty-nine white keys (or forty-nine total keys). If it's a tabletop electronic piano or synthesizer, be sure the instrument is on a table that allows enough room for your knees and thighs when you sit in front of it on a sturdy bench or straight-backed, armless chair. (Should your electronic keyboard be mounted on an adjustable stand, you may want to reposition it to a comfortable height.) Although Elton John and Jerry Lee Lewis can do acrobatics while playing the piano, it is a good idea to begin playing in a comfortable seated position.

If you are using a non-electric (or *acoustic*) piano, you must be sure your instrument is in tune before you begin to play. If the instrument has not been tuned in several months, chances are that you will need the services of a professional tuner. If you are using an electric piano or synthesizer, you can easily tune the instrument by adjusting the instrument's tuning control (refer to the manual for your instrument for detailed tuning instructions).

Notes on the Keyboard

Musical notes are named using the first seven letters of the alphabet. These letter names indicate notes in an ascending sequence—from low to high. After the final G note, the sequence begins again:

A—B—C—D—E—F—G, A—B—C—D—E—F—G, and so on.

A full-sized piano is able to repeat this pattern many times. Few other instruments offer the player so wide a range of notes—or the ability to play so many notes at one time.

The *black notes* of the piano occur in groups of two and three. The white key which occurs before every group of two black notes is a *C note*. The note labeled *Middle C* is the C note nearest to the center of the keyboard.

Middle C

Get into a comfortable playing position in front of the piano, find Middle C and play it once. Now, beginning at the lowest C note on your keyboard, find and play every C note in sequence, from lowest to highest. Notice that, although each new C note is obviously higher than the next, they all sound like different versions of the same note.

The white key which occurs before every group of three black notes is an *F note*. Play every F note on the keyboard, from lowest to highest.

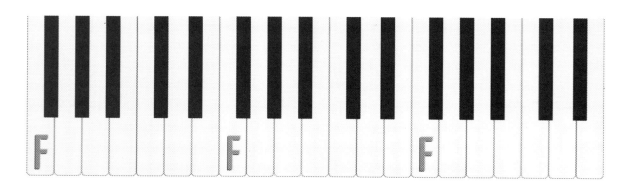

YOU CAN *play piano*

by Amy Appleby

*To my first and best piano teacher,
Dorothy Duncan*

Order No. AM 932349
US International Standard Book Number: 0.8256.1516.X
UK International Standard Book Number: 0.7119.5214.0

Exclusive Distributors:
Music Sales Corporation
257 Park Avenue South, New York, NY 10010 USA
Music Sales Limited
8/9 Frith Street, London W1V 5TZ England
Music Sales Pty. Limited
120 Rothschild Street, Rosebery, Sydney, NSW 2018, Australia

Printed and bound in the United States of America by
Vicks Lithograph and Printing

Amsco Publications
New York • London • Paris • Sydney

Table of Contents

As you can see, the black-note groupings provide the pianist with a frame of reference for locating and playing the white keys on the piano keyboard. In the keyboard diagram that follows, a *D note* occurs in the middle of every group of two black keys, an *E note* occurs immediately after every group of two black keys, and so on. Take the time to memorize the letter names of the white keys of the piano keyboard.

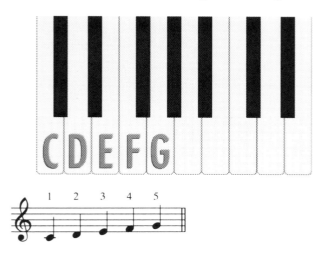

The Right Hand

The pianist makes most frequent use of the piano's *middle range.* Let's take a look at the some of the keys in this range. Place the thumb of your right hand on Middle C (as indicated by the finger number **1**). Place the fingers of your right hand (**2, 3, 4,** and **5**) on consecutive white keys, as shown. This hand position is called *C Position,* because the right thumb is placed on Middle C. Now, play these notes in sequence.

Play the same sequence backward, beginning with the right pinky (**5**) on the G note.

Play these two sequences together, beginning with the thumb (1).

Practice this *five-finger* exercise until you can play it evenly and smoothly. Here are some things to remember as you play.

• Keep your fingers curved and relaxed.
• Depress each key fully and firmly with the fingertips.
• Lift each finger just as the next finger goes down—so that each note has the same time value.

Notes on the Staff

Written music is a universal language of notes and symbols, arranged on the musical *staff* which consists of five lines and four spaces. Let's take another look at the five notes you have just played as they appear on the musical staff. Notice how the five notes of *C Position* progress by *steps* in alternating lines and spaces on the staff. Take a few minutes to memorize the letter names of these notes as they correspond to the notes on the staff.

The sign at the beginning of this staff is known as a *treble clef.* This clef is also called the *G clef,* because it curls around the second line of the staff—the position of the G note. This note serves as a point of reference for naming all other notes on the staff. In most piano music, the treble clef is used to mark the part played by the right hand. This hand is often responsible for playing the tune (or *melody*) of a piece. You'll find you can play the melody to many songs with these notes alone.

Rhythm Basics

Each note written on the staff not only tells you which key (or *pitch*) to play on the piano keyboard—but also how long the tone should last. The combined *note values* of a song melody form its *rhythm*.

The basic unit of rhythm in music is called a *beat*. Musical notes range in length from just a fraction of a beat to a duration of several beats. Once you are familiar with note values and musical counting, you'll be able sightread the melodies of hundreds of songs on your own.

Sometimes the term *rhythm* is used to describe the overall rhythmic "feel" or underlying "beat" of a song—as in "rock rhythm" or "Latin rhythm." You'll have the chance to explore these and other popular styles later on. The sections that follow focus on how notes are used to indicate rhythm in all types of written music. The best way to learn about rhythm is to play it—so get ready to play some great tunes as you master the basics of note values and musical time.

Basic Note Values

Familiarize yourself with the duration in beats of each of these basic note values. Notice how the notes are distinguished by the presence or absence of a line or *stem*—and by appearance of the dot (or *notehead*), which may be either outlined or filled-in.

♩ **Quarter Note** = 1 beat

♩ **Half Note** = 2 beats

𝅝 **Whole Note** = 4 beats

These basic note values form a pattern. The *half note* (which lasts for two beats) is twice the length of the *quarter note* (which lasts for one beat). Similarly, the *whole note* (four beats) is twice the length of the half note (two beats).

Take a look at the first phrase of the traditional melody "Jingle Bells," which contains each of these note values.

$\frac{4}{4}$ Time

One important key to the overall rhythm of a piece is the *time signature*, a numerical symbol which appears after the clef at the beginning of a piece of music, as shown. The time signature used in this example of "Jingle Bells" tells the pianist that the piece is written in $\frac{4}{4}$ *time* (pronounced "four-four time")

The top number of this time signature (4) indicates that there are four beats per measure—and the bottom number (4) indicates that a quarter note gets one beat. Sometimes the symbol c is used to indicate $\frac{4}{4}$ time.

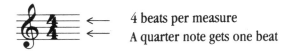

Barlines divide each *bar* (or *measure*) of the melody phrase into four equal beats (counted "**1**-**2**-**3**-4, **1**-**2**-**3**-4," and so on—with a stress on the first and third beat of each measure). A *double barline* marks the end of the excerpt.

Count each beat aloud as you clap the rhythm of "Jingle Bells"—that is, count out each beat number slowly and evenly, but clap only on the beats which correspond to notes of the melody (these beat numbers appear in boxes). Now place your right hand in C Position and play this phrase of "Jingle Bells," beginning with the third finger on the E note. Count each beat as you play.

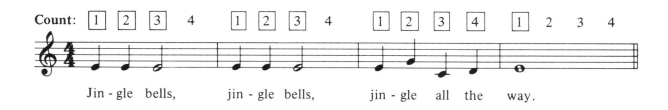

Eighth Notes

Many tunes contain short notes that are worth only one-half of a beat. These notes are called *eighth notes*.

 **Eighth Note** = ¹/₂ beat

Eighth notes often occur in groups of two or more. Each group is linked with a bar or *beam*. Count the rhythm of this example aloud. Note that eighth notes are counted with the word "and" between beats in the second measure—as indicated by the ampersand sign (**&**) between numerals in the example below.

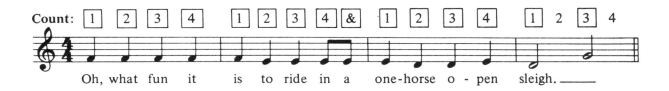

Now count and clap the rhythm in the second phrase of "Jingle Bells." Remember to count each beat number aloud slowly and evenly, but clap only on the beats which appear in boxes.

Place your right hand in C Position and play the full chorus of "Jingle Bells," beginning with the third finger on the E note. Practice "Jingle Bells" (without counting) until you know it well—and can play it with confidence at a moderate speed.

Jingle Bells

Oh, what fun it is to ride in a one-horse o - pen sleigh.____

Jin - gle bells, jin - gle bells, jin - gle all the way.

Oh, what fun it is to ride in a one-horse o - pen sleigh.

Sightreading a Song Melody

Reading music (or *sightreading*) is an important skill for any pianist. The best way to develop your sightreading abilities is to learn new songs.

At this point, you are ready to sightread any melody in C Position. Position the thumb of your right hand on Middle C and play the theme of Beethoven's "Ode to Joy" slowly and evenly—beginning with the third finger on the E note.

Practice "Ode to Joy" until you can play it with ease and confidence at a moderate speed (or *tempo*). After you warm up the left hand in the next section, you can add harmony to this beautiful theme.

Ode to Joy

The Left Hand

In most piano music, the left hand is responsible for playing the background (or *harmony*) of a piece. The clef used to mark music for the left hand is called the *bass clef*. This clef is also known as the *F clef*, because it curls around the fourth line up from the bottom of the staff—and highlights this line with two dots. This marks the position of the F note, which serves as a point of reference for naming all other notes on the staff.

Place the pinky of your left hand on *Low C* (which is the C note below *Middle C*). Play these notes in sequence, beginning with the pinky (**5**) on Low C.

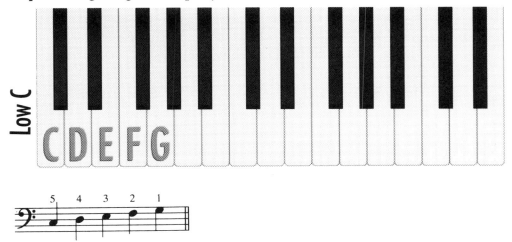

Play this sequence backward, beginning with the thumb (**1**) on the G note.

Now play these two sequences together, beginning with the pinky (**5**) on Low C.

Playing the Harmony

Most piano music is written on the *grand staff,* which is made up of the treble staff and the bass staff, linked together by *a brace.*

Take a look at "Ode to Joy," as noted on the grand staff. The staff with the treble clef on top features the melody, which is played by the right hand. The bass staff below shows music played by the left hand, the harmony part.

Place your left hand in C Position—with the pinky (5) on the C note below Middle C. Now practice the left hand part of "Ode to Joy." Remember, each whole note lasts for four beats. The half notes in the last measure each last for two beats. Count 1-2-3-4 evenly aloud as you play the left-hand part.

Once you are familiar with the left-hand part of "Ode to Joy," try putting it together with the right-hand part. Play this piece at a slow, even pace until you are quite familiar with it.

Ode to Joy

The C Major Scale

So far, you've practiced five tones—C, D, E, F, and G. Three more notes are needed to form the *C major scale*—A, B, and the C note above Middle C.

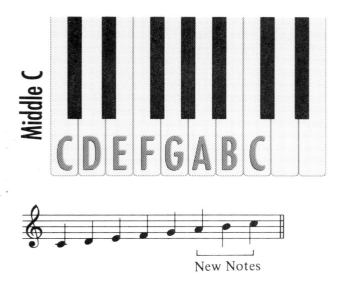

New Notes

Notice how the C major scale begins and ends on a C note—and contains eight tones. The distance between the two C notes is called an *octave.* The two C notes themselves form an *interval of an octave.*

To practice the new notes, place your right hand in *G Position,* as shown. This position features one more new note—the D—which is played with the right pinky. Now play this five-finger exercise with your right hand.

This is the C major scale in bass clef. The new notes are the same—A, B, and C. Note that the top C note in this scale is actually Middle C.

New Notes

Practice playing these new notes with your left hand in *G Position.* This position includes one more new key—the D note—which is played by the left thumb. Play this five-finger exercise, beginning with the left pinky on the G note.

You are already familiar with Beethoven's "Ode to Joy" in C Position. Now try this piece in G Position. First practice the melody with the right hand beginning with the third finger (**3**) on the B note. Then add the left-hand part, beginning with the left pinky (**5**) on G.

Ode to Joy

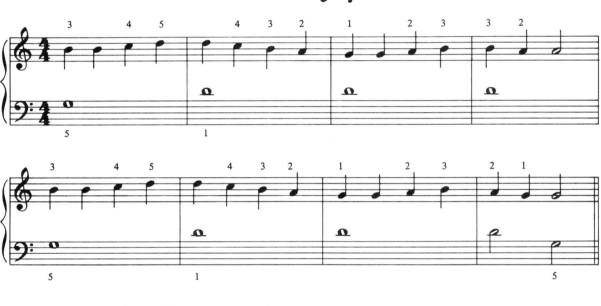

Extended Hand Position

Many song melodies extend beyond a single five-finger hand position—and require that pianists stretch their fingers up or down the keyboard to reach certain notes. Practice this exercise with the right hand, using an extended version of G Position. Notice that the B note is skipped—and your third, fourth, and fifth fingers must now stretch up one key to play the pattern, which features a new note at the top—the E note. As you play the songs that follow, you will learn many new notes—and chords, too. For your easy reference, these are listed in the "Table of Notes" or "Table of Chords" provided at the end of the book.

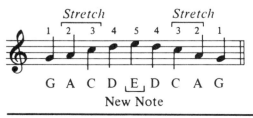

Get ready to play the tune "Tom Dooley" with your right hand in G Position, beginning with your thumb (**1**) on the G note. This traditional American song was a number one hit for the Kingston Trio in 1958—and remained on the pop charts for eighteen weeks. Be sure to stretch upward to play the first and last lines of this song. Note also the two eighth notes on the second beat of each line or *phrase* of the song's melody.

Once you are familiar with the melody of "Tom Dooley," add the harmony with the left hand in G Position (beginning with the second finger on the C note). Be aware that the half notes in the left-hand part change every two beats—while the whole note in the last measure should be held for four beats.

Tom Dooley

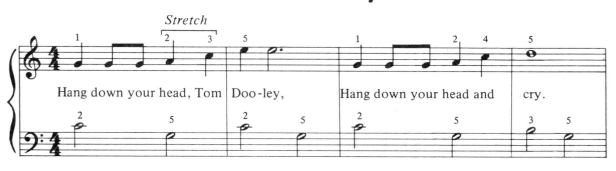

Hang down your head, Tom Doo-ley, Hang down your head and cry.

Hang down your head, Tom Doo-ley, Poor boy you're bound to die.

Chord Basics

A *chord* is a group of two or more notes which are played together. A three-note chord is called a *triad*. You'll find that you can play hundreds of different songs by learning just a few chords. This section will teach you the basic chord forms that musicians use to read lead sheets and create their own piano arrangements. Learning chords is an important first step to "playing by ear." Once you know how to play a few chords, you'll be able to figure out the harmony to many different songs on your own.

Let's look at how the eight tones of the C major scale are used to form basic triads in the *key of C major.* Note that the eight triads are marked with Roman numerals—and that the last chord is actually just a higher version of the I chord. (You'll learn more about the individual qualities of these basic chords later on.) Using the thumb, middle finger, and pinky of your right hand, play each of these chords in sequence up the scale, as shown. Note the finger numbers at the left of each chord. The top note of the **VII chord** is a new note—**F.** The top note of the last **I chord** is also a new note—**G.**

I　　II　　III　　IV　　V　　VI　　VII　　I

Now position your left pinky on Low C and play these five chords with the left hand.

I　　II　　III　　IV　　V

The C and G Chords

Most pop and rock songs only use a few basic chords. Once you know a few, you should experiment with them and learn how they work with different melodies.

The two most important chords in any key are the *I chord* and *V chord* (pronounced "one chord" and "five chord"). As their names imply, these chords are built on the first and fifth degrees of the scale. In the key of C, the I chord and V chord are called the *C chord* and *G chord,* respectively, to correspond with the letter name of the lowest note or *root* of the triad.

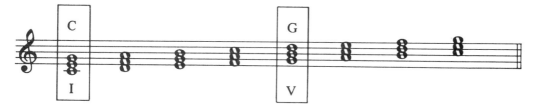

Note that, in each chord, the lowest note is called the *root* of the chord, the middle note is called the *third* of the chord, and the top note is called the *fifth* of the chord. Normally, these tones are played by the pianist's first, third, and fifth fingers. Here's how the C and G chords are noted for the left hand in bass clef.

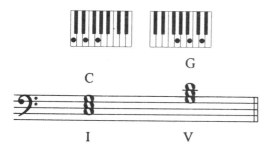

I　　V

Chord Inversion

In order to make it easy to alternate between the C and G chords with the left hand, let's rearrange the notes of the C triad so that the fifth of the chord (or G note) is played as the bass note of the triad, as shown—and the first and third (C and E) are moved up one octave. When the notes of a triad are rearranged in this way, the chord is called an *inversion.*

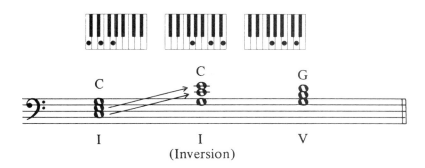

Practice these chords with the left hand until you can play them evenly and smoothly. Allow each chord to last for four beats.

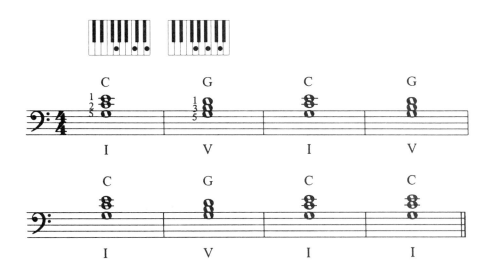

You'll be surprised at how many songs you will be able to play with just these two chords. Here's a piano arrangement of "Tom Dooley." Practice the left-hand part first. Let each chord last for four beats. Note that the chord symbols **C** and **G** are shown above the staff to indicate the chords played by the left hand. The corresponding Roman numeral chord symbols, **I** and **V** are listed below the staff for your reference. Once you are familiar with the left-hand part, play "Tom Dooley" with both hands together.

Tom Dooley

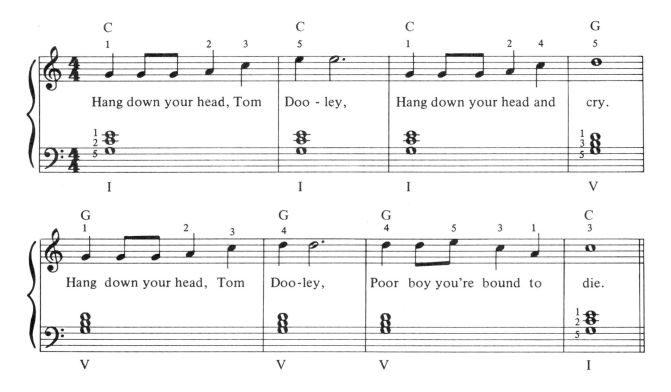

The G7 Chord

If you add or change one or more chord tones of a triad, you create an *altered chord*. The V chord is often altered by adding the seventh tone above the root tone. The resulting chord is known as a *V7 chord*. In the key of C, this chord is called the *G7 chord*. Here are the C and G7 chords in treble clef.

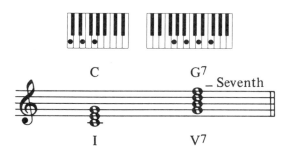

In order to make it easy to play the C and G7 chords in one position, the G7 chord should be rearranged to form this inversion. The third of the chord becomes the bass note, and the fifth of the chord is omitted.

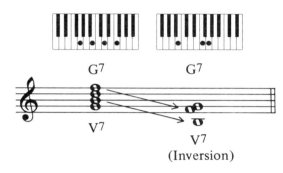

Here are the C and G7 chords in a bass clef exercise. Practice playing these chords with the left hand. Finger the V7 chord with your left pinky, index finger, and thumb (**5**, **2**, and **1**). Hold each chord for four beats.

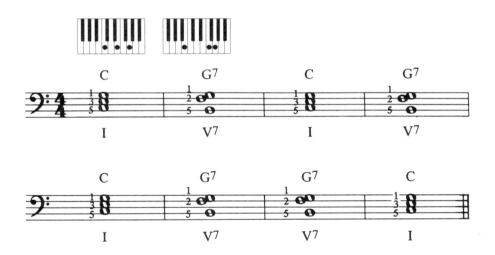

Once you can play this exercise smoothly, take a look at "Go Tell Aunt Rhody." Practice the melody first with your right hand. When you feel familiar with the melody, add the chords with the left hand.

Go Tell Aunt Rhody

The F Chord

The *F chord* is built on the fourth note of the C scale—so this chord is considered the *IV chord* in the key of C. Like the C and G chords, the F chord is made up of a root, third, and fifth.

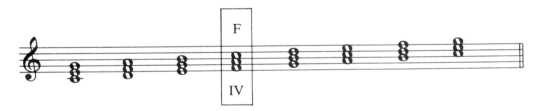

This inversion of the F chord (with the fifth of the triad moved to the lowest position) makes it convenient to play the F chord with the C and G7 chords.

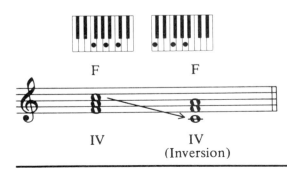

Here's the F chord in bass clef. Note the pinky plays the C note, while the index finger and thumb must stretch up to play the F and A notes, respectively.

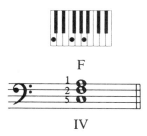

This chord exercise contains the C, G7, and F chords (the I, V7, and IV chords in the key of C). Practice the exercise with the left hand until you can play it evenly.

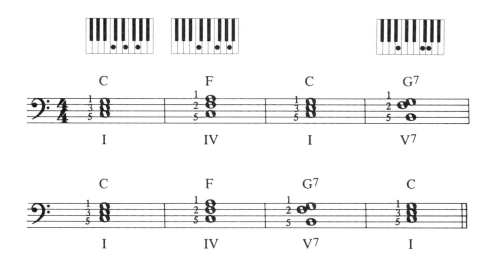

Once you are familiar with this exercise, play "Jingle Bells" with both hands. (The right hand begins with the third finger on the E note.)

Jingle Bells

Jin - gle bells, jin - gle bells, jin - gle all the way.

Oh, what fun it | is to ride in a | one-horse, o - pen | sleigh. _____

Jin - gle bells, | jin - gle bells, | jin - gle all the | way.

Oh, what fun it | is to ride in a | one-horse, o - pen | sleigh.

Rests

Most music is composed of sounds and silences. The silent beats in music are represented by signs called *rests.* Rests are named and valued in correspondence with the note values you learned previously.

Whole Note = Whole Rest = 4 Beats

Half Note = Half Rest = 2 Beats

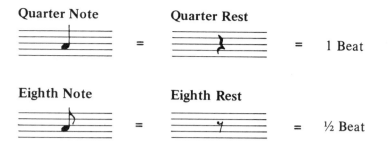

Rests and notes may be combined in the same measure, as long as their combined values add up to the correct number of beats (in this example, four beats to a measure). Count the beats of this phrase as you clap the rhythm of the notes.

Now play "Old MacDonald" with the right hand. Be sure to allow the appropriate number of silent beats where the rests occur in the melody. The fingering numbers will show you where you need to stretch your hand position to play the melody.

Old MacDonald

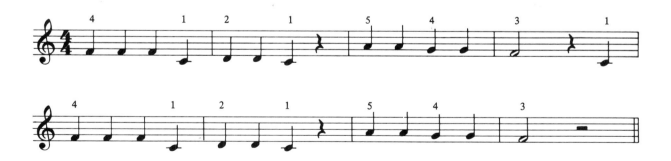

Pickup Notes

Certain song melodies require an incomplete first measure to provide for a *pickup,* which is simply a note or notes that occur before the first stressed beat of the song. When a musical composition features a partial measure containing a pickup, it usually makes up the remaining beats of the first measure in the last measure of the piece. This means that the last measure of the piece will also be incomplete.

You can see a pickup at work in "Polly-Wolly Doodle." There's a one-beat pickup at the beginning of the song and three beats in the final measure. Taken together, the pickup and the last measure add up to four beats—the number of beats required in a complete measure of a piece in $\frac{4}{4}$ time. Count aloud as you play the melody of this song with the right hand, beginning with the thumb on the C note. There's a new note for the right hand in this melody—the B note. You'll need to move down your thumb to play this new note (which is the white key below Middle C).

Once you are familiar with the right-hand part, play the piece with both hands together, as written. (The left-hand part features the familiar C and G7 chords.)

Polly Wolly Doodle

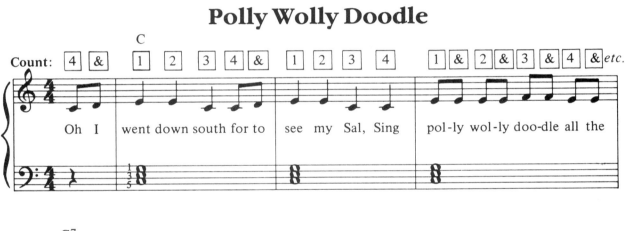

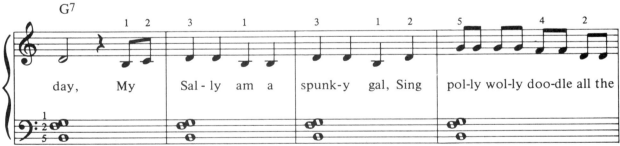

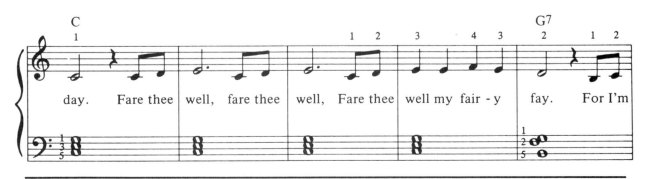

goin' to Lou-si-a-na for to | see my Sus-i-an-na, Sing | pol-ly wol-ly doo-dle all | day.

Ties and Slurs

A *tie* is a curved line which links two or more notes of the same pitch. This indicates that a tone be held for the combined length of the two tied notes. In this excerpt from "Careless Love," a tie links a whole note (four beats) and a half note (two beats). That means that the final C note should last for a total of six beats.

Love, oh love, oh care - less love,_____

A *slur* is a curved line connecting two or more notes of varying pitch. This mark indicates that the notes be played or sung in an especially smooth and connected manner (called *legato*). In this excerpt from Edward Elgar's "Pomp and Circumstance" slurs are used to indicate legato playing.

A slur is always necessary in a song melody when two or more notes share one syllable of lyric, as shown in this passage from "(I Wish I Was in) Dixie."

I ___ wish I was __ in the land of cot - ton,

Because of their similar appearance, ties are often confused with slurs. The way to tell them apart is to remember that ties link notes of the same pitch, while slurs always link notes of varying pitch.

This arrangement of "The Banks of the Ohio" features ties and slurs. Practice the right-hand part until you can play it with ease. Remember, some slurs are necessary only because of a shared syllable in the lyric—and require no special attention on the part of the pianist. This type of slur occurs in "The Banks of the Ohio" at the words "a" and "flow." Any additional slurs direct you to play the indicated notes legato (smoothly). Such a slur occurs in the left-hand part in the last measure. Here the C chord should be smoothly played note by note. (You'll get more practice with this note-by-note technique when you study "Arpeggios.")

The left-hand part of "The Banks of the Ohio" features half-note and whole-note chords. Practice these chords in rhythm, and then play this classic ballad with both hands.

The Banks of the Ohio

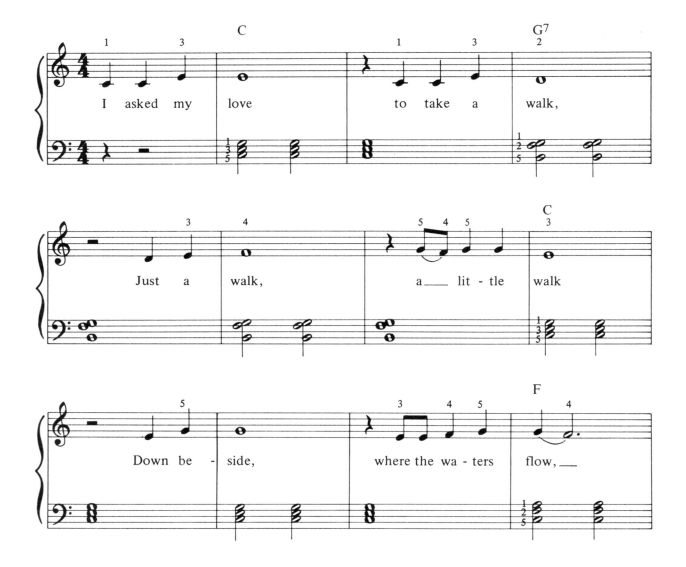

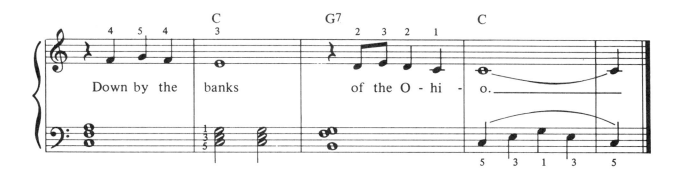

Repeats, Intros, and Endings

Most styles of music call for their individual sections to be repeated at times. In fact, this kind of repetition usually serves to strengthen the overall structure of a given song. Two dots before a double bar form a *repeat sign.* If this sign occurs at the end of the piece, it indicates that you should repeat the entire piece once from the beginning. Play "Hot Cross Buns" twice through in tempo.

If a repeat sign occurs in the middle of a piece, go back to the beginning and repeat the section before going on.

If a mirror image of the repeat sign occurs earlier in the piece, the performer should only repeat from that point onward. This version of "Hot Cross Buns" has a pickup measure at the beginning. The inverted repeat sign indicates that you should skip this measure when you repeat the piece.

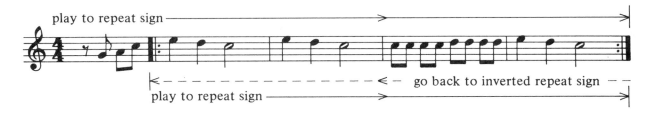

Many song arrangements feature added music at the beginning of a piece called an *intro* (short for *introduction*). Other arrangements feature added music to be played after the final verse of a piece (an *ending*). This version of "Hot Cross Buns" features an intro—as well as a first and second ending. The introduction and first ending are played the first time through the piece—and the second ending is played when the piece is repeated.

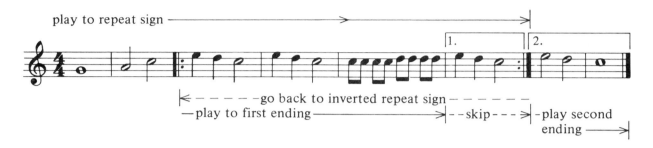

Now play "Kumbaya," which features an introduction and second ending. The first ending is played at the end of the first verse, while the second ending is played at the end of the second and final verse.

Kumbaya

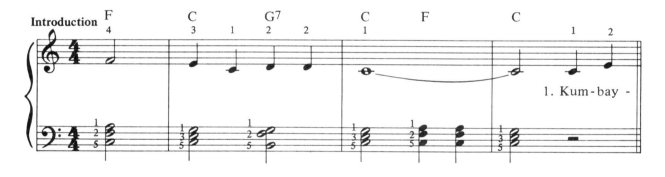

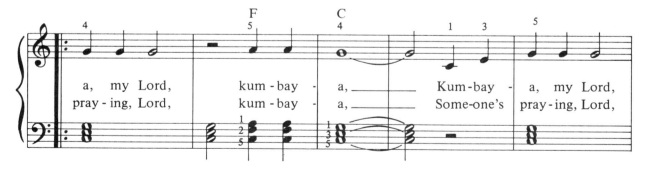

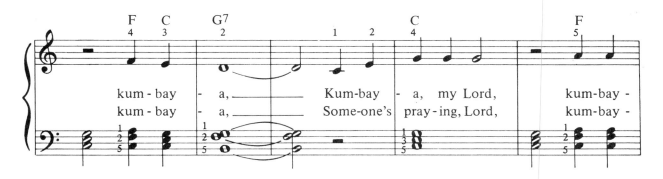

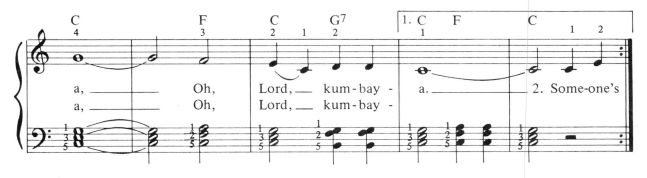

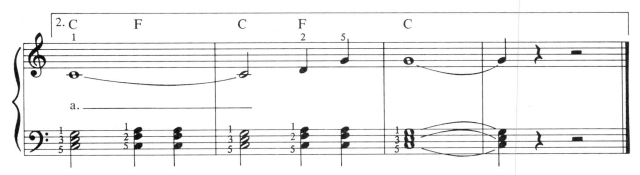

Dotted Notes and Rests

A dot placed after any note means that it should last one-and-a-half times its normal duration. For example, if you add a dot after a half note (which normally lasts two beats), you get a *dotted half note*, which lasts for three beats.

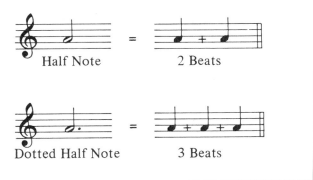

In the same way, when a dot is placed after a quarter note (which normally lasts one beat), a *dotted quarter note* results—which lasts for one-and-a-half beats.

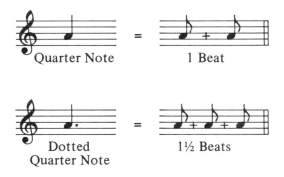

Clap and count "Angels We Have Heard on High," as shown.

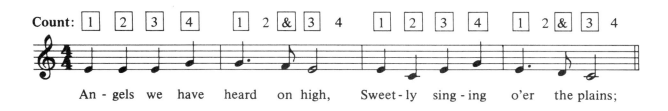

As with notes, when a dot is placed after any rest it means that the rest should last one-and-a-half times its normal duration. If you add a dot after a quarter rest (which normally lasts one beat), a *dotted quarter rest* results (which lasts for one-and-a-half beats).

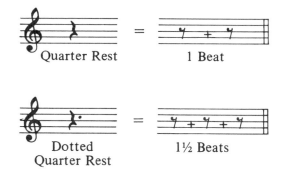

It's easy to understand dotted notes and rests when you compare them with the regular note and rest values you have already learned.

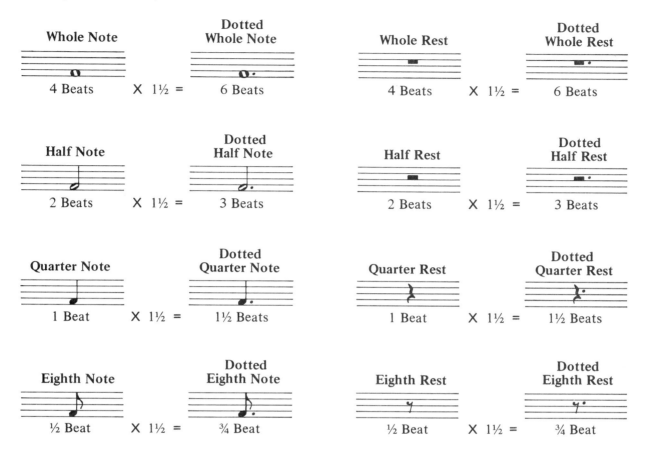

Whole Note	Dotted Whole Note	Whole Rest	Dotted Whole Rest
4 Beats X 1½ =	6 Beats	4 Beats X 1½ =	6 Beats

Half Note	Dotted Half Note	Half Rest	Dotted Half Rest
2 Beats X 1½ =	3 Beats	2 Beats X 1½ =	3 Beats

Quarter Note	Dotted Quarter Note	Quarter Rest	Dotted Quarter Rest
1 Beat X 1½ =	1½ Beats	1 Beat X 1½ =	1½ Beats

Eighth Note	Dotted Eighth Note	Eighth Rest	Dotted Eighth Rest
½ Beat X 1½ =	¾ Beat	½ Beat X 1½ =	¾ Beat

Take the time to memorize the appearance and value of each dotted note and rest. Then count and clap the first line of "Oh, Susanna"—a song by Stephen C. Foster which James Taylor made even more famous on his well-known pop album, *Sweet Baby James*. Notice that the dotted quarter and eighth note is a repeating pattern in the melody line—and a dotted half note occurs at the end of each phrase of the song. Practice the right-hand part of this piece. Then play "Oh, Susanna" using both hands.

Oh, Susanna

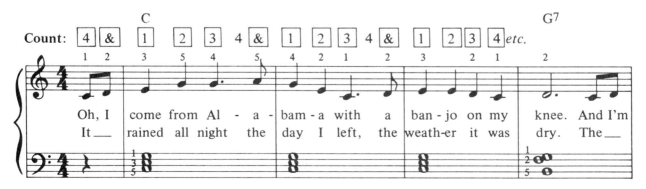

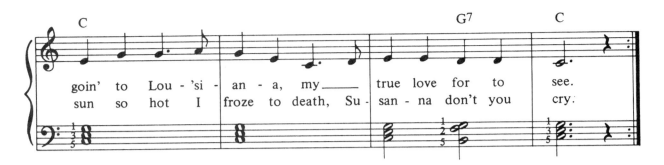

goin' to Lou - 'si - an - a, my _____ true love for to see.
sun so hot I froze to death, Su - san - na don't you cry.

Oh, Su - san - na, oh, don't you cry for me. For I

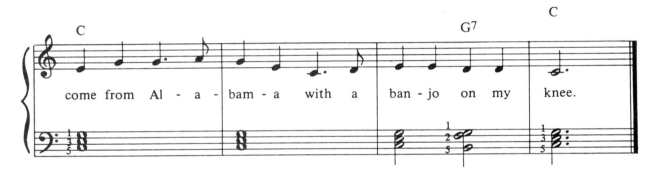

come from Al - a - bam - a with a ban - jo on my knee.

$\frac{3}{4}$ Time

Each of the songs you have played so far has been in $\frac{4}{4}$ time—that is, with four beats to the measure. Many songs are written in $\frac{3}{4}$ *time* ("three-four time")—also called *waltz time*—with three beats to a measure.

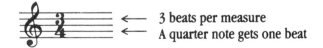

← 3 beats per measure
← A quarter note gets one beat

Play "Drink to Me Only With Thine Eyes," as you count the indicated beats ("**1**-2-3, **1**-2-3," and so on—with a stress on the first beat of every measure). Note that when two dotted half notes are tied together (as occurs in the last measure of this song) the total note value is six beats. Also note that in $\frac{3}{4}$ time, the whole rest has a duration of three beats (not four beats, as in $\frac{4}{4}$ time). Just remember that a whole rest lasts for the "whole" measure, regardless of the time signature.

Drink to Me Only With Thine Eyes

Broken Chords

You can add movement and power to a song by using *broken chords* in the harmony part. In this example, the root or bass tone of each chord is separated from the third and fifth of the chord. With the left hand, practice this pattern of broken chords at a slow tempo until you can play it smoothly.

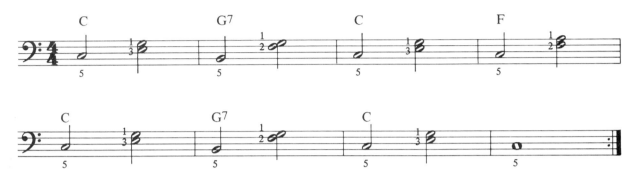

Now play "When the Saints Go Marching In." This familiar American spiritual was a popular hit for Bill Haley, who gave it a rock beat and retitled it "The Saints Rock 'N Roll." Here, broken chords give this tune a distinctive rhythm. Notice that the last measure only has one beat—so, when you repeat the song, it forms a complete measure with the three-beat pickup at the beginning.

When the Saints Go Marching In

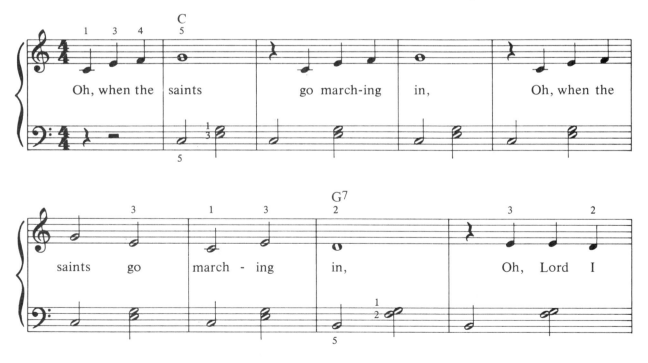

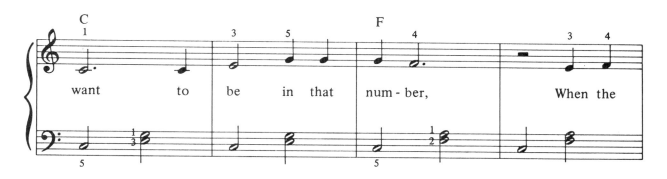

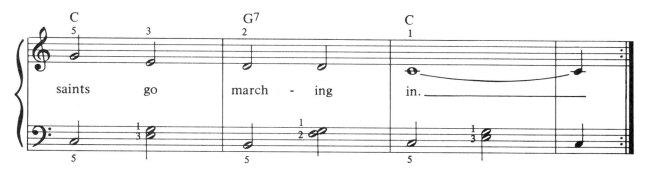

Arpeggios and Rolled Chords

An *arpeggio* is simply a chord that is broken into single notes. This technique is frequently used in classical, pop, and rock music to add texture to the harmony. Composers and arrangers have long explored the many effects that may be achieved with arpeggios—notably their continuous and soothing effect. Play this arpeggio exercise with the left hand.

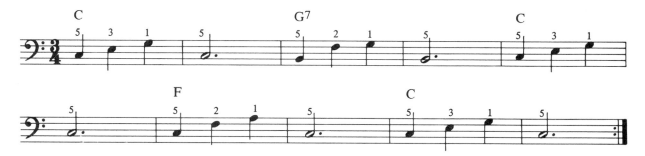

Sometimes arpeggios are meant to be played as quickly as possible. This kind of arpeggio is called a *rolled chord*. The zig-zag marking to the left of each chord in this left-hand exercise indicates that you arpeggiate (or *roll*) the notes of the chord quickly, from the bottom note up. Be sure to hold each key down as it is played so that the chord will continue to sound for three beats.

Now play the traditional favorite, "Down in the Valley," which features rolled chords in the first verse and arpeggios in the refrain.

Down in the Valley

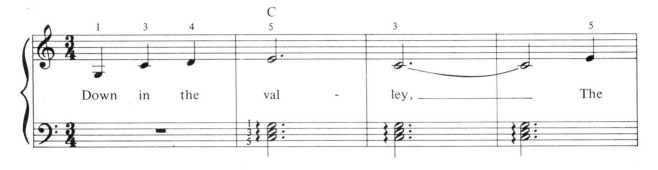

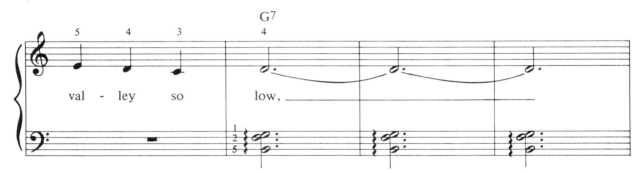

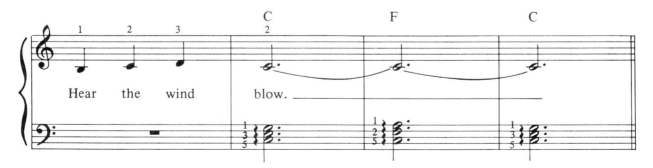

Refrain

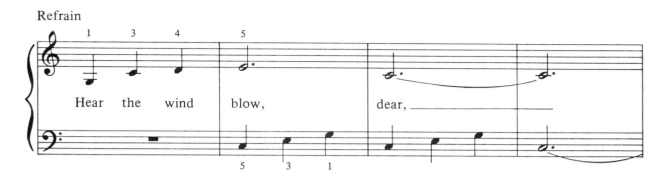

Hear the wind blow, dear,

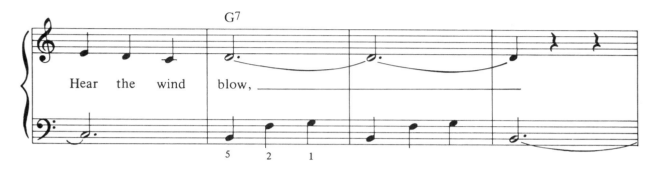

G7

Hear the wind blow,

Hang your head o - ver,

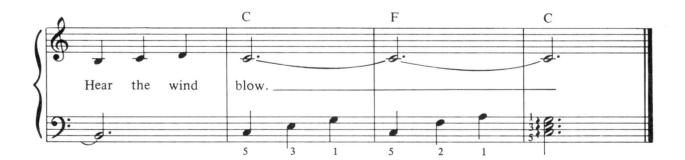

C   F   C

Hear the wind blow.

$\frac{6}{8}$ Time

Some time signatures call for the eighth note to last for one beat (instead of the usual quarter-note beat). Take a look at the time signature in $\frac{6}{8}$ time.

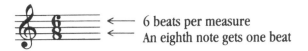

As you can see, there are six beats to the measure, with an eighth note valued at one beat. In $\frac{6}{8}$ time, a stressed beat occurs every three eighth-note beats, providing two stresses in every measure. This is illustrated by boldface numbers in the first phrase of "The Irish Washerwoman." (As you can see, $\frac{6}{8}$ time has much of the same rhythmic feeling as $\frac{3}{4}$ time, with a stress on every third beat.)

Now combine your knowledge of $\frac{6}{8}$ time and dotted notes as you play "For He's a Jolly Good Fellow."

For He's a Jolly Good Fellow

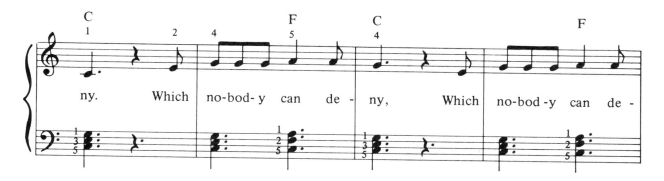

ny. Which no-bod-y can de - ny, Which no-bod-y can de -

ny. For he's a jol-ly good fel - low, For he's a jol-ly good

fel - low, For he's a jol-ly good fel - low, Which no-bod-y can de - ny.

Triplets

Composers and arrangers sometimes need to divide a basic note value into three notes of equal value. These three notes are collectively called a *triplet,* which is indicated by the numeral *3* above the notes. A quarter-note triplet normally lasts for two beats—and is noted with a numeral *3* within a bracket. (The "quarter notes" in this triplet are actually each worth two-thirds of a beat.)

An eighth-note triplet normally lasts one beat—and is noted with a numeral *3* above the *beam* that links the three notes together. (The "eighth-notes" in this triplet are each worth one-third of one beat.)

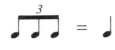

Triplets add a certain stately beauty to the powerful hymn, "Amazing Grace." Clap and count the first line of this song using the words "three-and-ah" to correspond with the triplet in the first measure.

As a tribute to the lasting popularity of this song, Judy Collins made it a top-40 hit in 1971. The following year, the Royal Scots Dragoon Guards of Scotland's armored regiment recorded a bagpipe band version of this tune that put it back on the pop charts. Practice the right-hand part of this tune before adding the chords with the left hand. The fingering numbers indicate where you should stretch or reposition your fingers. Play this one at a slow tempo.

Amazing Grace

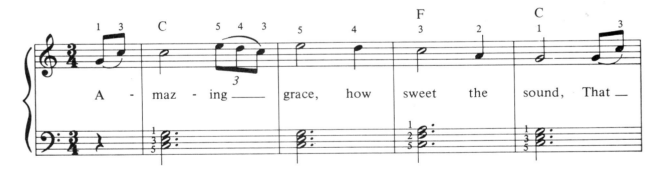

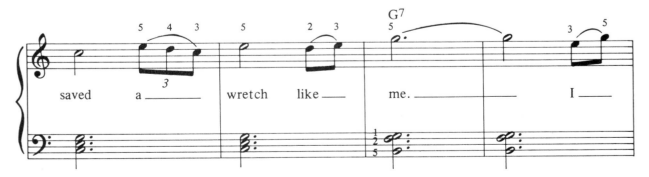

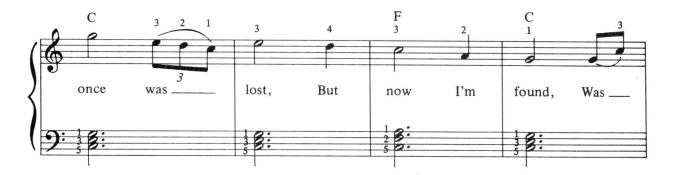

once was _____ lost, But now I'm found, Was _____

blind but _____ now I see. _____

Sixteenth Notes

A *sixteenth note* is a short note which lasts for only a quarter of a beat. Here's how it fits in with the note values you have already learned.

As you know, eighth notes are counted with the word "and" between beats—as indicated by the ampersand sign (**&**) between numerals. The eighth notes in this example are counted "one-and-two-and-three-and-four-and." You'll need additional syllables to count the rhythm of sixteenth notes, which are counted "one-ee-and-ah, two-ee-and-ah, three-ee-and-ah, four-ee-and-ah." Count and clap this rhythm exercise.

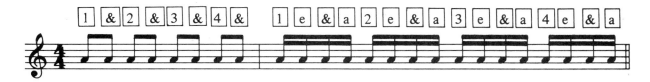

Count and clap the opening phrases of "Listen to the Mockingbird." Note that the first four sixteenth notes form a one-beat pickup (counted "four-ee-and-ah").

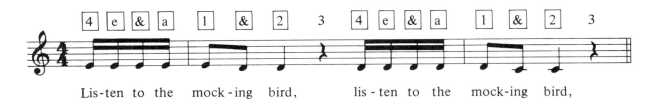

Sixteenth notes are often paired with dotted eighth notes in song melodies. This pattern gives a characteristic lilting rhythm, as in the popular hit, "Wimoweh." This traditional South African Zulu song (retitled "The Lion Sleeps Tonight") became a number one hit for the Tokens (featuring Neil Sedaka) in 1961. Robert John put it back on the charts for 13 weeks in 1972.

Practice the melody of this song with your right hand, then add the left-hand part.

Wimoweh

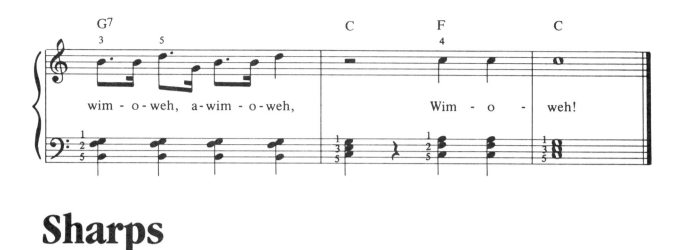

wim - o - weh, a - wim - o - weh,   Wim - o - weh!

Sharps

So far, you've played several songs using the white keys of the piano keyboard: A, B, C, D, E, F, and G. As you may have already noticed, the black keys of the piano keyboard provide pitches in between these notes. These pitches are called *sharp* or *flat notes,* depending on their musical context. The names of these notes are formed by adding a *sharp sign* (♯) or *flat sign* (♭) after the note letter name. These signs, as well as the notes themselves, are often simply called *sharps* and *flats.* The white-key notes are some-times called *natural notes* (or *naturals*) to distinguish them from sharps or flats. Take a look at the sequence of the natural and sharp notes as they occur on the piano keyboard.

As you can see, each sharp key occurs just above the white key with the same letter name. Thus, the black note in between the C and D notes is labeled *C♯*, the black note in between the D and E keys is *D♯*, and so on. Notice that no sharp occurs between the E and F keys—and none occurs between the B and C keys. This sequence of natural and sharp notes is known as the *chromatic scale.* Here's how the scale looks on the musical staff in both treble and bass clef.

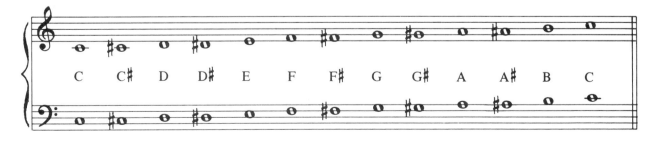

C   C♯   D   D♯   E   F   F♯   G   G♯   A   A♯   B   C

Take the time to memorize the position and name of each of the sharp notes as they appear on the keyboard and staff. It's also important to remember that if a note appears with a sharp sign, all subsequent notes of that measure in the same position on the staff are also sharped, as indicated in this example. (The barline cancels the sharp sign, so the final note is an A natural.)

The following arrangement of the traditional Jewish folksong, "Havah Nagilah," features an octave accompaniment. You'll have to stretch your left hand quite a bit to play this part. Practice this octave exercise with left pinky and thumb.

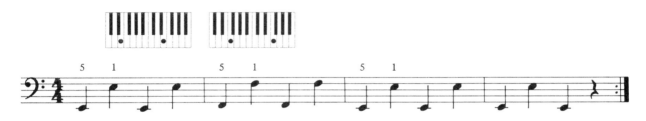

Several G♯ notes occur in the melody of "Havah Nagilah." Be aware that the second note in the third measure (corresponding with the syllable "-vah") is also a G♯ note. This G♯ is not cancelled by the barline because it is tied over into the next measure. Practice the right-hand part of this traditional hora, then play the piece twice through with the indicated endings.

Havah Nagilah

Flats

In certain musical contexts, the black keys of the piano are viewed as *flat notes* rather than sharp notes. Take a look at the sequence of the natural and flat notes as they occur on the piano keyboard.

As you can see, flat notes occur one key lower than the white key of the same letter name on the piano keyboard. The flat sign appears after the letter name of the lowered white key to indicate the black-key name. Thus, the black-key note in between the C and D notes is labeled *D♭*, the black-key note in between the D and E keys is *E♭*, and so on. As with sharps, no flat occurs between the E and F keys—and none occurs between the B and C keys.

This descending version of the chromatic scale features natural notes and flats.

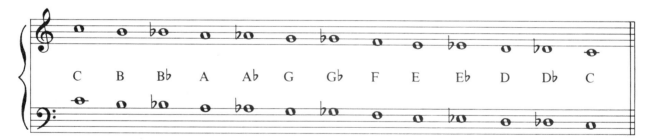

Take the time to memorize the name and position of each of these flat notes as they appear on the keyboard and staff. Also remember that if a note appears with a flat sign, all subsequent notes of that measure in the same position on the staff are also flatted, as indicated in this example. (The barline cancels the flat sign, so the final note is an A natural.)

"Rock Island Line" was a top-10 hit for Lonnie Donegan in 1956. The right-hand part of this memorable tune features an E♭ note. Practice the melody of "Rock Island Line," then add the chords with the left hand.

Rock Island Line

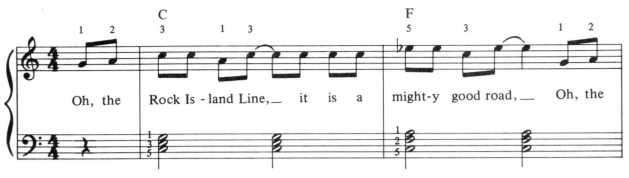

Oh, the Rock Is - land Line, __ it is a might-y good road, __ Oh, the

Rock Is - land Line, __ it is the road to ride, Oh, the

Rock Is - land Line, __ it is a might - y good road, __ If you

want to ride it, got to ride it like you find it, Get your

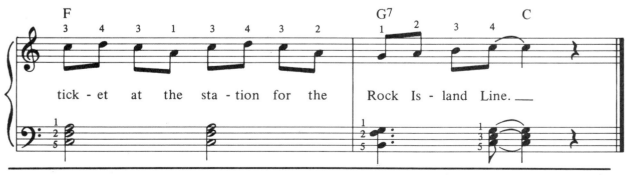

tick - et at the sta - tion for the Rock Is - land Line. __

Naturals

Naturals are notes played on the white keys of the piano. A *natural sign* cancels a sharp or flat sign that has appeared with a note of the same position. Once a natural sign has been used, all other subsequent notes in the same position on the staff in that measure are affected by the natural sign.

    A   A♯   A   A

As you might expect, a natural sign may be cancelled by a flat or sharp sign with a note of the same position in the same measure. (Notice that the barline then cancels the sharp.)

    A   A♯   A   A♯   A

Some pieces contain both sharps and flats. Whether a note is flatted or sharped depends on its particular musical function in the piece. But, as a general rule, an accidental that leads up to a natural note is written as a sharp note—and an accidental that leads down to a natural note is written as a flat note. This rule is illustrated in this excerpt from "My Melancholy Baby."

Come to   me   my   mel - an - chol - y   ba -   by,

With your right hand, play the melody of "The Old Grey Mare," which features naturals and sharps. Once you are familiar with the melody, add the chords with your left hand.

The Old Grey Mare

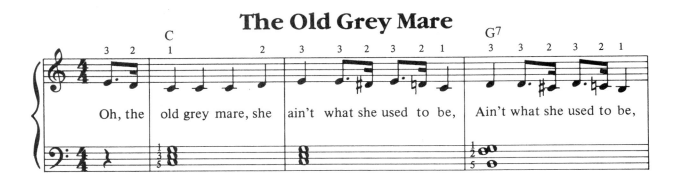

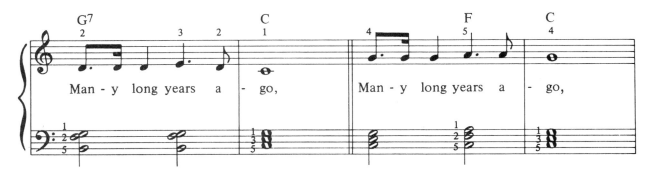

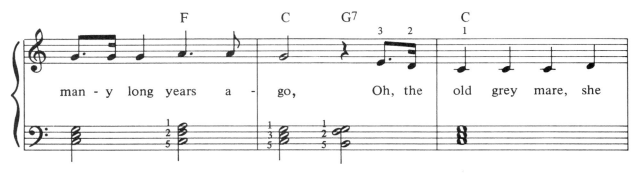

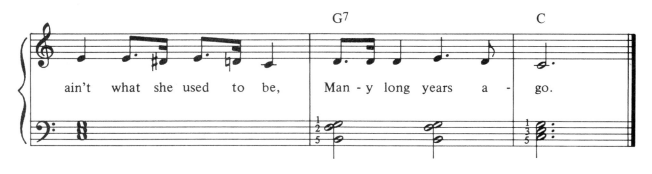

The C7 Chord

The *C7 chord* is simply a C major chord with an added B♭ note—the flatted seventh degree of the C major scale. (This chord is also called the I7 chord in the key of C major).

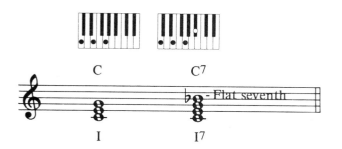

Here are the C, C7, F, and G7 chords noted in bass clef for the left hand. Notice that the G note is not included in the C7 chord (so you can play it using three fingers). Practice playing these chords in sequence.

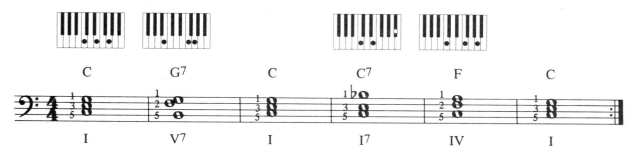

Once you are familiar with the chord exercise, practice the left-hand part of the favorite college song, "Goodnight Ladies." Then add the melody part with the right hand. Once you've played "Goodnight Ladies" (which contains the C7 and G7 chords), turn to the "Table of Chords" in the back of the book to practice playing all the other seventh chords (D7, E7, F7, A7, and so on).

Goodnight Ladies

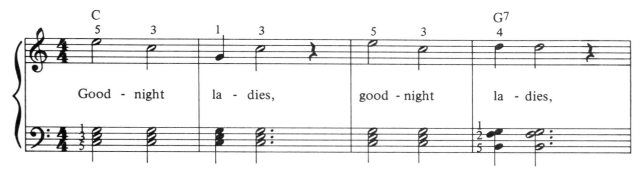

Good - night la - dies, we're go - ing to leave you now.

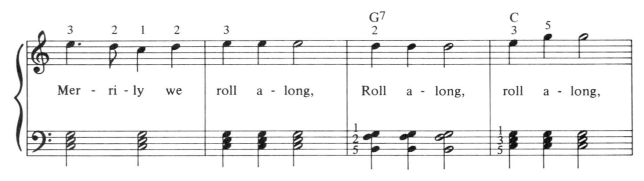

Mer - ri - ly we roll a - long, Roll a - long, roll a - long,

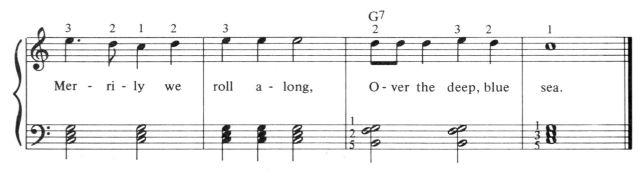

Mer - ri - ly we roll a - long, O - ver the deep, blue sea.

Minor Chords

So far, you've learned the important major chords in the key of C. The triads which occur on the second and sixth degree of the scale in any key are important *minor chords*. These are noted **IIm** and **VIm**, respectively—and correspond with the Dm and Am chords in the key of C, as shown.

A listing of all major and minor chords for all keys is included in a comprehensive "Table of Chords" at the end of this book. Take the time to practice all of the major and minor chords included in this chart. As you learn these chords, you'll soon see that a minor chord is simply formed by altering one note of the corresponding major chord—that is, the third of the major chord is lowered by one half step. Compare the D major and D minor chords.

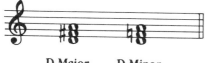

D Major D Minor

Minor chords often add a certain sad or introspective quality to a song—and can add the perfect touch to a love ballad (or any song that creates a personal portrait or calls up visions of the past). This arrangement of "Molly Malone" (also known as "Cockles and Mussels") features the Dm, C, Am, F, G, and G7 chords (the IIm, I, VIm, IV, V, and V7 chords in the key of C). Note that the Dm chord only appears in the intro section of the piece—while the Am chord is included in this recurring chord pattern: C, Am, F, G. Practice this chord exercise.

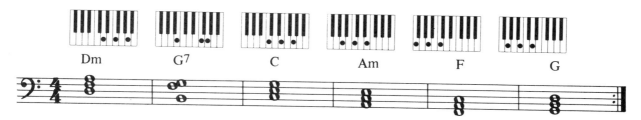

Now practice the left-hand part of "Molly Malone," which features broken chords. Once you are familiar with the harmony of the song, add the melody with the right hand. (Finger numbering in the melody part will guide you to the correct hand positions. You'll see that it's sometimes necessary to switch fingers when playing repeated notes, as in measures 9 and 10.) Notice how the minor chords add to the sentimental quality of this traditional favorite.

Molly Malone

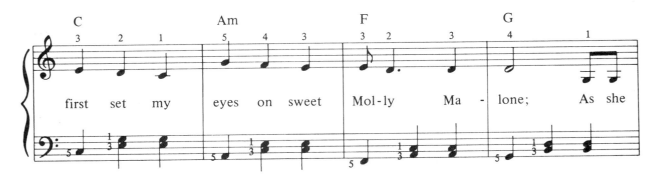

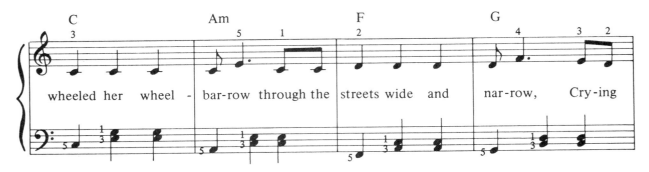

Tempo

Composers and arrangers often indicate approximately how fast a piece should be performed by using an Italian or English term on top of the staff at the beginning of a piece or section. Here are some of the more common Italian tempo markings and their English equivalents. These terms indicate the overall speed of a piece or section of music.

Lento (or **Largo**) = Very slow
Adagio = Slow
Andante = Walking pace
Moderato = Medium
Allegretto = Medium fast
Allegro = Fast
Presto = Very fast
Prestissimo = As fast as possible

Variations in tempo within a piece are often used to provide contrast in music, particularly in longer works. Sometimes a composer or arranger wishes to indicate that the regular beat or tempo of a piece should hold or pause for a moment on a specific note or rest. This hold or pause is indicated with a *fermata* (⌒). (The amount of time that the indicated note or rest should be held is left to the discretion of the performer.)

Certain terms call for a changing of the tempo. The term *ritardando* (often abbreviated as *ritard.* or *rit.*) indicates that the tempo should slow down. *Accelerando* calls for a quickening of the tempo. The term *a tempo* (pronounced ''ah tempo'') tells the musician to return to the normal speed of the piece.

''Danny Boy'' is a traditional Irish ballad that has been recorded by a range of different stars—from Bing Crosby to Conway Twitty. Twitty's 1959 recording of this beautiful tune enjoyed thirteen weeks on the pop charts, peaking in tenth position.

This arrangement of ''Danny Boy'' features octave arpeggios in the harmony part. Practice this chord exercise with your left hand.

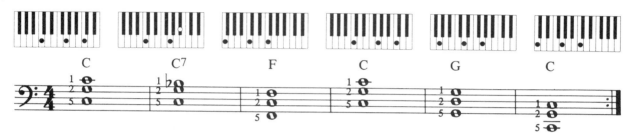

As you practice the right-hand part of ''Danny Boy,'' you'll see that you need to cross your third finger over your thumb in measures 3, 11, and 30. In measure 28, you should cross your thumb underneath your index finger. Note also that, in measure 6, both thumbs play the melody note—Middle C. Once you are familiar with the melody, play ''Danny Boy'' using both hands. Notice the overall tempo is adagio (slow)— and that fermatas and ritardandos add much to the song's emotional power.

Danny Boy

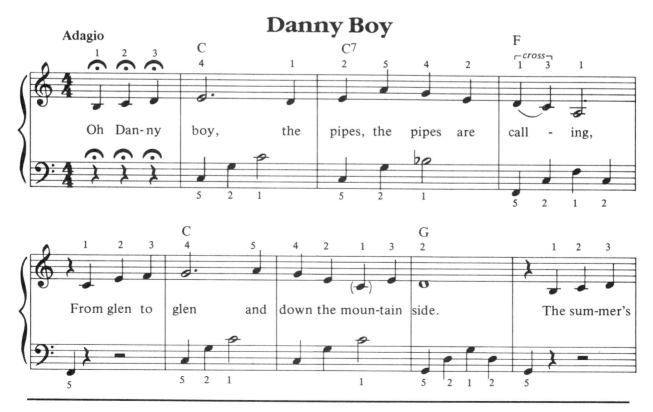

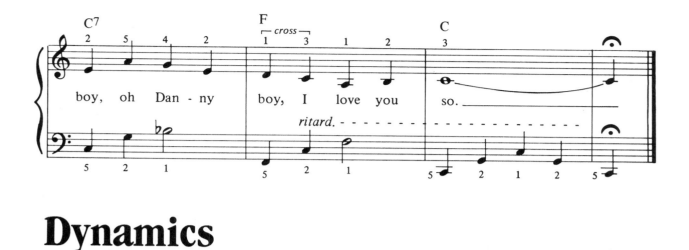

boy, oh Dan - ny boy, I love you so.

Dynamics

Volume is an important factor in all piano performance—and the patterns of volume in a particular composition or performance are called its *dynamics*. (If you are playing an electronic keyboard or synthesizer that does not have a volume pedal, you'll need to adjust the master volume control to vary the dynamics in a piece.)

Terms or symbols that indicate volume are called *dynamic markings.* Italian or English words may be used at the beginning of a piece to indicate overall volume. Symbols are often used to abbreviate these words, especially to indicate volume changes during the piece. Take the time to memorize these common dynamic symbols and their corresponding meanings in Italian and English.

pp = **Pianissimo** = Very soft
p = **Piano** = Soft
mp = **Mezzo piano** = Moderately soft
mf = **Mezzo forte** = Moderately loud
f = **Forte** = Loud
ff = **Fortissimo** = Very loud

Sometimes a composer or arranger wishes to indicate a gradual change in volume at a specific point in the piece. An increase in volume is called *crescendo*—and is indicated by a *crescendo marking.* Begin softly (and gradually get louder) as you play this five-finger exercise.

A decrease in volume is called a *diminuendo*—and is indicated by a *diminuendo marking.* Begin loudly (and gradually get softer) as you play this five-finger exercise.

"Hail! Hail! the Gang's All Here" is a rousing song that is often performed with dramatic changes in volume. This arrangement of the song features soft (*p*), loud (*f*), and very loud (*ff*) passages. Use these dynamics as you play the piece—and be sure to get gradually louder at the end, as indicated by the crescendo symbol.

Hail! Hail! the Gang's All Here

The Key of C Major

Composers and arrangers write music in different keys to bring out the best in a particular composition or musical instrument. For the pianist, some keys are easier to play in than others. Using different keys for the individual sections or songs in a larger work—such as a symphony or a Broadway show—adds variety to a performance. This is important to remember if you are planning your own concert, or writing music for others to perform.

Many pieces of music require that certain notes be sharped or flatted as a general rule. The number of sharps or flats which occur regularly in a piece of music determines the *key*. Rather than writing in a sharp or flat sign every time one should occur, these signs are written in a *key signature* at the beginning of each staff.

Most of the musical examples in the book so far have been written in the *key of C major*, which has no sharps or flats. As you know, all the notes of the C major scale occur on the white keys of the piano keyboard. Once you understand the construction of the scale in the key of C major, you'll be able to build the scale and key signature for every other major key.

The shortest distance between two notes, is called a *half step*. A *whole step* is the equivalent of two half steps. Let's examine the pattern of whole steps and half steps in the C major scale. Take the time to memorize this important pattern, because it is the blueprint for all other major scales.

C Major Scale

In order to play the C major scale smoothly with your right hand, you'll need to cross your thumb under your third finger going up the scale. When you come down the scale, cross your third finger over your thumb. Practice the scale exercise above until you can play it smoothly and evenly.

"Michael, Row the Boat Ashore" was a number one hit for the Highwaymen in 1961. This arrangement features the C, F, and G7 chords (the familiar I, IV, and V7 chords in the key of C).

Michael, Row the Boat Ashore

The Key of G Major

Once you are quite familiar with the step-by-step pattern of the C major scale, take a look at the *G major scale*. The notes of this scale are the building blocks for music in the *key of G major*. Notice that this scale requires an F♯ note in order to follow the proper step-by-step pattern for major scales. Practice this scale using the indicated fingering.

G Major Scale

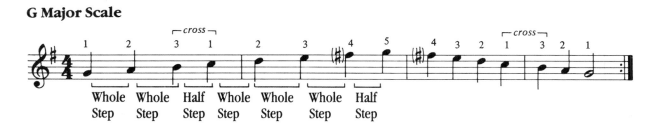

Since the F♯ note is a regular feature in the key of G major, it is represented in the key signature after the clef on every staff of the piece. This means that all notes that occur in the F Position in the piece (unless otherwise marked) will be sharped in the key of G. (This applies to all F♯ notes in the piece, no matter how high or low.) The key signature is notated on the treble and bass staves as follows.

Here are the G, C, and D7 chords (the I, IV, and V7 chords in the key of G, respectively). The D7 chord is a new one for you—and requires an F♯ note. Play each of these chords in sequence with the left hand.

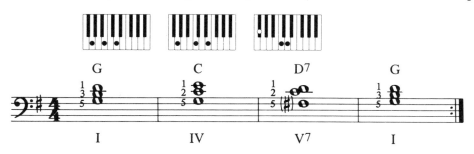

Now play "Michael, Row the Boat Ashore" in the key of G Major.

Michael, Row the Boat Ashore (Key of G Major)

jah. Mi-chael, row the boat a - shore, Hal-le - lu - jah.

The Keys of D and A Major

Once you know the step-by-step pattern used to form all major scales, its easy to play in any major key. In this and the next sections, you'll explore major keys that are common in piano music—and easy to play. You'll get a chance to play in these keys in the "Developing Your Repertoire" section.

Practice each of these major scales and chord patterns using the indicated fingering. (Here, courtesy accidentals are provided in parentheses to remind you of the flats or sharps that appear in the key signature.)

D Major Scale

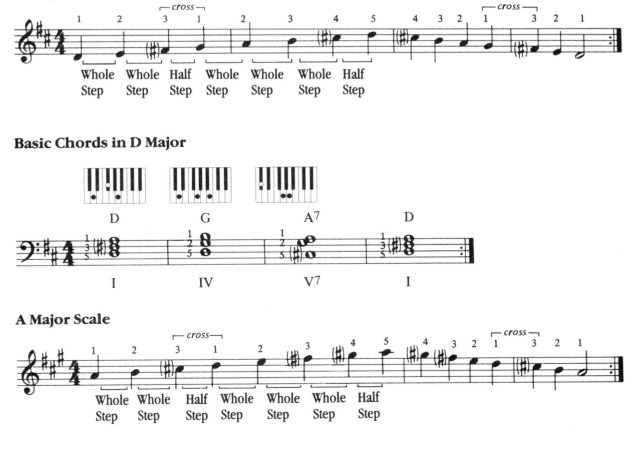

Basic Chords in D Major

A Major Scale

Basic Chords in A Major

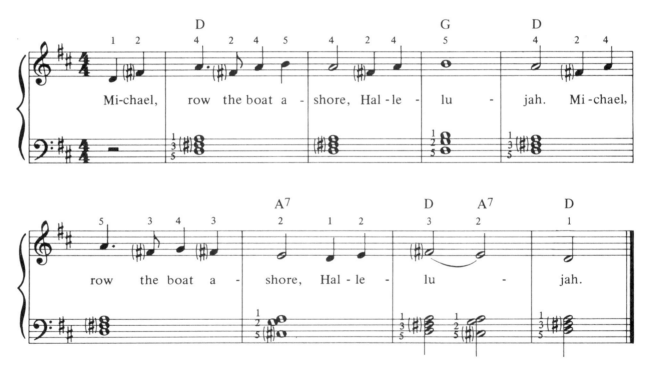

Now play "Michael, Row the Boat Ashore" in the keys of D Major and A Major.

Michael, Row the Boat Ashore (Key of D Major)

Mi-chael, row the boat a - shore, Hal-le - lu - jah. Mi-chael,

row the boat a - shore, Hal-le - lu - jah.

Michael, Row the Boat Ashore (Key of A Major)

Mi-chael, row the boat a - shore, Hal-le - lu - jah. Mi-chael,

row   the boat   a - shore,   Hal - le - lu - jah.

The Keys of F and B♭ Major

Now let's focus on the key signatures that contain flats. Here's the F major scale, which features one flat—and the B♭ major scale, with two flats. Practice each of these major scales and basic chord patterns using the indicated fingering.

F Major Scale

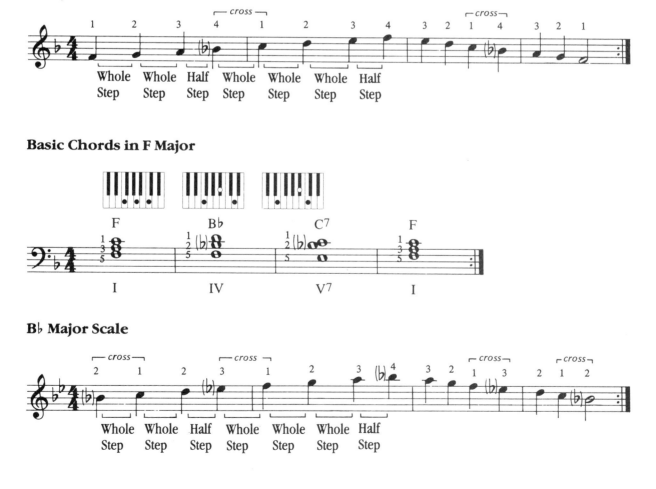

Basic Chords in F Major

B♭ Major Scale

Basic Chords in B♭ Major

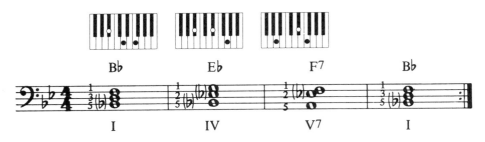

Now play "Michael, Row the Boat Ashore" in the keys of F Major and B♭ Major.

Michael, Row the Boat Ashore (Key of F Major)

Mi-chael, row the boat a - shore, Hal - le - lu - jah. Mi-chael,

row the boat a - shore, Hal - le - lu - jah.

Michael, Row the Boat Ashore (Key of B♭ Major)

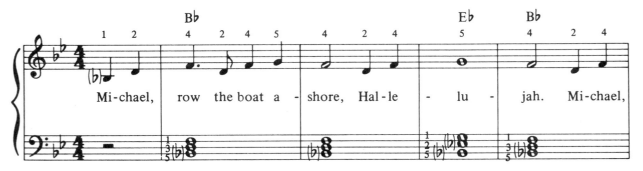

Mi-chael, row the boat a - shore, Hal - le - lu - jah. Mi-chael,

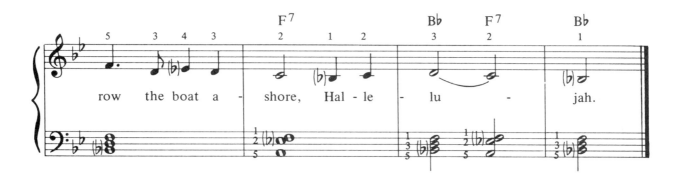

row the boat a - shore, Hal - le - lu - jah.

Minor Keys

As you know, music may be written in different keys to accommodate the ranges of particular voices or instruments. Another reason for writing a piece in a particular key is to lend a special tonal color, or *tonality,* to a piece. Many of the musical excerpts you have studied in this book so far have been written in a major key, and therefore have major tonalities. Sometimes a composer chooses to use a *minor key* to lend a dark, introspective, or sad quality to a piece. A minor key is formed by lowering certain notes of the corresponding major scale (usually the third, sixth, and seventh scale degrees).

You really don't need to know all the technical rules regarding minor keys in order to play in them. Just pay attention to the flats (or sharps) indicated in the key signature when you play the song—just as you would when playing in a major key.

In the earlier section, "Minor Chords," you learned that a minor triad is formed by lowering the third of the corresponding major chord. The folk favorite "The Erie Canal" is written here in the key of C minor— with three flats in the key signature (B♭, E♭, and A♭). In this song, the B♭ note is always made a natural by an accidental.

The left-hand part of "The Erie Canal" features the C minor, F minor, and G7 chords (the I minor, IV minor, and V7 chords). Practice these three chords in sequence with the left hand. Be sure to include the E♭ note and A♭ note, as indicated by courtesy accidentals in parentheses—and use B natural instead of B♭.

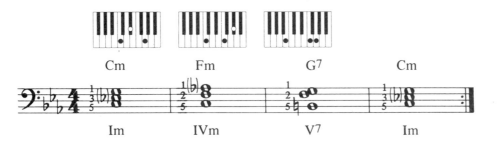

The melody of "The Erie Canal" features a lowered third (the E♭ note) and lowered sixth (the A♭ note). Courtesy accidentals are provided in parentheses in the first two measures only. After that, you'll have to watch out for these flat notes on your own. Practice the melody with your right hand until you can play it with ease. Then play the song using both hands. The minor key gives "Erie Canal" a mournful sound. Remember to slow down somewhat when you reach the *ritard.* at the end of the piece.

The Erie Canal

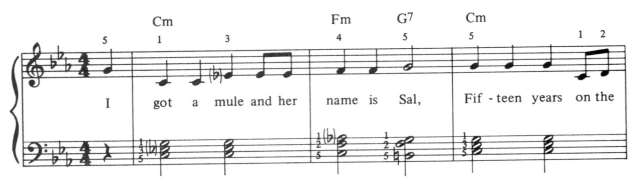

Developing Your Repertoire

Now that you've got the basics of piano playing under your belt, you're ready to start adding songs to your *repertoire*—which is simply the list of songs that you can play with confidence. In fact, learning new songs is the most enjoyable way for a developing pianist to strengthen playing skills and explore new territory on the piano. If you plan to perform for others, it's a good idea to memorize some of the songs in your repertoire—or have your sheet music well-organized and easily accessible when you're ready to perform.

In the sections that follow, you'll find piano arrangements for hit songs in all musical styles—including blues, rock, pop, jazz, and classical. As you play the songs in these sections, you'll use skills you learned in previous sections. You will also learn new piano techniques that will add style to your playing. Even if you have a special interest in only one or two types of music—you'll find that you will benefit from playing songs in each section.

Once you've played through all of the arrangements in these sections, select three that you'd like to focus on as performance pieces. Set aside some time each day to practice these songs. Work on the exercise that goes with each piece before you play it. Practice each song until you can play it easily and confidently at a steady tempo. Fingering numbers above the notes will guide you to the stretches you need to make during each piece. If you encounter any notes or chords which you do not know, refer to the "Table of Notes" or "Table of Chords" at the back of this book.

As you develop your repertoire, you may wish to allocate part of your practice time to singing and playing. It's also great practice to get together for sessions with friends who sing or play other instruments.

The Blues

The blues was born in the American South. It evolved from the work songs written by Black-American slaves before the Civil War—and so bears the influence of African rhythms and tonality. The blues is known for its power to evoke the listener's emotions—because its lyric often tells a personal story of troubles and longing. The plaintive melody and harmony of the blues, coupled with its strong and simple rhythm, make it a universally appealing musical form.

Most blues melodies and solos are based on the *pentatonic blues scale.* This scale has only five notes per octave (instead of seven, as found in the major and minor scales). Notice the *blue notes* are lowered by one half-step with flats. These notes correspond to the flatted third and seventh degrees of the major scale. These two blue notes give the blues that dark and mournful sound.

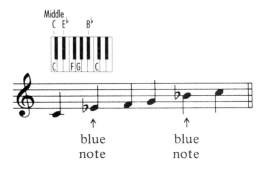

Play this blues scale exercise, using your right hand. Remember to cross your thumb under your third finger on the way up the scale—and then cross your third finger over your thumb on the way down the scale.

Many traditional blues songs and modern blues-rock tunes are written in *twelve-bar blues* form— with twelve bars (or measures) of music in each complete verse of the song. The vocal line is often stated in three phrases per verse (with four bars in each phrase), as shown.

Well, good morning blues, blues how do you do?
Well, good morning blues, blues how do you do?
Well, I'm doing all right, good morning, how are you?

The repetition and simplicity of the twelve-bar blues form is the secret to its penetrating power and lasting popularity.

Good Morning Blues

"Good Morning Blues" is a classic twelve-bar blues song that has been recorded by many of the great blues masters. This tune features the standard blues chords—I7, IV7, and V7. In the key of C, these chords are C7, F7, and G7. Practice this blues chord exercise with your left hand.

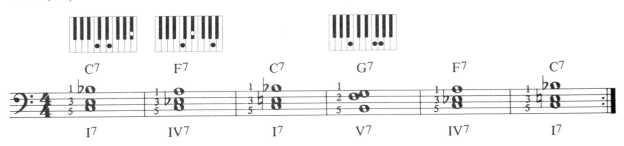

Blues pianists know that a hard-driving sense of rhythm is what makes a great blues performance. Count aloud as you play this characteristic rhythm with the left hand. Notice that the second chord in measures three and four jumps in a little early to add some excitement to the blues beat. This important rhythmic technique (called *syncopation*) is a trademark of the blues—and an integral feature of jazz as well.

Once you are familiar with this exercise, play the melody to "Good Morning Blues" with the right hand. Notice how the last note of the melody (which occurs on the word "you") jumps in a little early to create a bluesy syncopation. Once you are familiar with the melody, play this classic song using both hands.

Good Morning Blues

Frankie and Johnny

"Frankie and Johnny" is perhaps the most famous blues of all time. This stark tale of love and murder was recorded by many great blues artists—and was a signature tune for Mae West. As a testament to this song's versatility, R&B singer/songwriter Brook Benton put it on the charts for four weeks in 1961; soul singer Sam Cooke put it on the charts for seven weeks in 1963; and Elvis Presley, the king of rock and roll, made it a hit once again for five weeks in 1966.

Practice this chord pattern with your left hand.

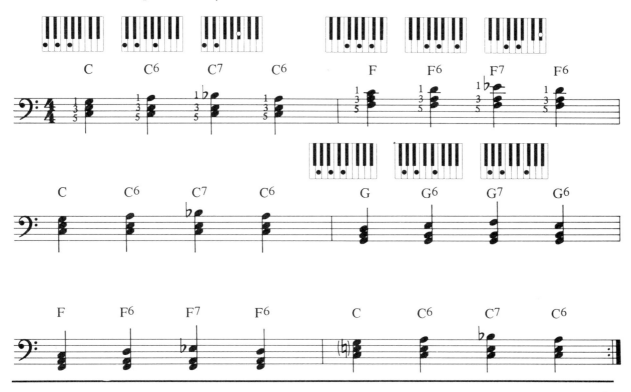

Now play this jazzy chord—the C13♯11—using both hands.

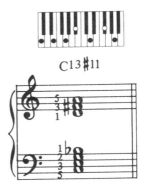

C13♯11

Practice the melody part of "Frankie and Johnny" with your right hand. Then play the song with both hands together. Use the first ending for all verses (except the final verse, which takes the second ending). Be sure to roll the final C13♯11 chord from the bottom up.

Frankie and Johnny

Frank-ie and John - ny were lov - ers. Oh, Lord-y how__ they could

love. Swore to be true __ to each oth - er,

True as the stars a - bove; He was her man, ___

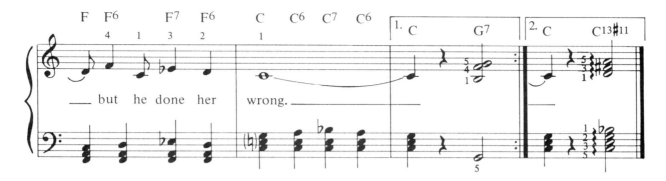

but he done her wrong. _____

Rock

Rock and roll emerged in the 1950s as "rockabilly" music—a blending of hillbilly-style country music and the driving beat of Black rhythm & blues. Rock's pioneers include Bill Haley, Carl Perkins, Chuck Berry, Elvis Presley, Jerry Lee Lewis, and Little Richard. By the late 1950s, rock and roll was no longer a novelty, but had entered the pop mainstream—with millions of avid fans in American and Europe.

In the 1960s, the popularity of rock music was brought to a new peak with the advent of British rock groups, beginning with the Beatles. Other British groups, like the Who and the Rolling Stones, followed soon after. Today, rock and roll is the predominant musical style on the pop charts. Other rock forms have also developed over the years, including acid rock, glitter rock, southern rock, and heavy metal. In general terms, today's mainstream rock music features electronic instrumentation with guitar and vocals—and a hard-driving, constant beat. A *rock ballad* is really any rock tune that has a relatively slow tempo.

In this section, you'll get to play some classic rock uptunes and ballads—hits by Cream, the Animals, and Los Lobos. As you perform each of these tunes, you'll see the close relationship between rock and its parent forms—blues and rhythm & blues.

C.C. Rider

"C.C. Rider" is an all-time favorite blues and rock hit that has been performed by a range of artists. Ma Rainey brought this tune to position fourteen on the charts in 1925. In 1957, rhythm and blues singer Chuck Willis had a career-making hit with this song—and inspired the dance craze called "The Stroll." In 1963, rhythm and blues singer LaVern Baker recorded her hit version of this tune (entitled "See See Rider"). The magic had still not worn off this terrific rhythm number—for Eric Burdon & the Animals made "See See Rider" a hit once again for seven weeks in 1966.

Before you try "C.C. Rider," practice this chord exercise with your right hand.

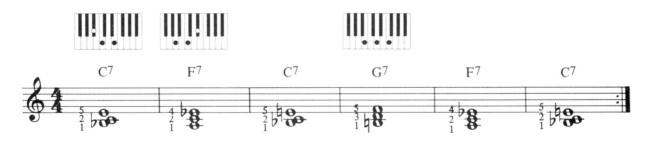

Now practice the left-hand part of "C.C. Rider" until you can play it with confidence at a steady rock beat. Then play the tune using both hands together.

C.C. Rider

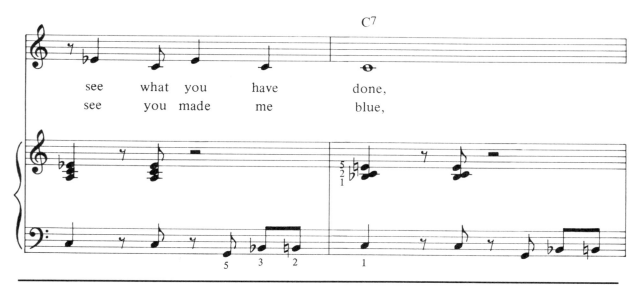

Crossroads

"Crossroads" is a traditional blues tune that Cream turned into a rock and roll hit in 1969. Originally entitled "Crossroad Blues," this song was a favorite of blues master Robert Johnson. Here's a blues-rock version of "Crossroads" that brings out its driving beat.

Before you play "Crossroads," practice the rhythmic bassline played by the left hand in the introduction. Although there are three sharps in the key signature, you won't use any black keys for this exercise. The G natural note is a blue note in this key (the key of A major)—and adds to the riff's hip sound. Remember to place added stress on the first note, as indicated by the *accent mark* ($>$). Count aloud as you play this exercise with the left hand.

After you are familiar with this bassline, take the time to practice it at twice the speed, as noted below.

Once you've got the introduction down, practice this right-hand exercise. Notice that your right hand moves from an extended C Position to A Position as you play the melody—and that the last note of the C-Position phrase is played on a black note—C♯.

The first phrase of "Crossroads" has a syncopated rhythm in the second measure to create a blues-rock feel. Use your right hand to play the first phrase of this tune as you count the indicated beats. This rhythmic pattern is a recurring theme in the melody of "Crossroads."

Now play "Crossroads" at a slow and even tempo using both hands. Remember to keep the repeating octaves played by the left hand strong and steady. Once you can play the tune with confidence at a moderate speed, try playing it at a fast rock tempo.

Crossroads

Introduction

1. I went

Verse

down to the cross - roads, fell down on ___ my
there at the cross - roads, tried to flag ___ a

knees, I went
ride, Stand-in'

D7

down to the cross - roads, fell down on ___ my
there at the cross - roads, tried to flag ___ a

A7

knees, I asked the
ride, No - bod - y

La Bamba

Latin rock and roll star Ritchie Valens made a hit with "La Bamba" in 1959. The movie based on his life, *La Bamba,* was released in 1987—with music by the Latin-American rock quintet Los Lobos. Their version of this terrific Latin tune held the number one position on the charts for three weeks.

Practice the left- and right-hand parts separately before you play this one—then play it with both hands together. Once you can play "La Bamba" at a moderate tempo with ease, work to play the tune at a fast and steady beat. Place some added stress on the first and third beats of every measure—and you'll bring out the Latin flavor of this terrific dance tune.

La Bamba

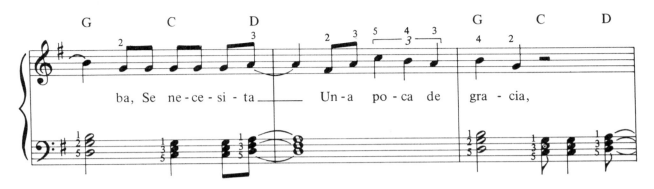

Pop

Generally speaking, any song or instrumental piece which enjoys wide commercial popularity is considered "pop" music—and the relative success of a pop song is measured by its rank on the pop charts.

The term *pop* music is more specifically used to refer to any music which features contemporary lyrics, standard chord patterns, bright vocals, and electronic instrumentation. Pop music differs from rock and roll in that it does not traditionally feature a jarring beat, pitch-bending, or raw vocal and instrumental parts.

Contemporary pop and rock musics developed during the 1950s. Early pop music took several forms: there were "doo-wop" groups (like the Marcels and the Five Satins); close-harmony vocal ensembles (like the Supremes and Shirelles); and close-harmony groups doing "surf" music (notably, the Beach Boys and Jan and Dean).

Throughout the sixties and seventies, pop drew more and more influence from rock music—and today, many pop chart hits are actually rock, pop-rock, or "soft" rock music. The music of pop artists like Prince, Madonna, and Michael Jackson combines the harmonious and bright qualities of pop music with the driving beat, bold instrumentation, and special effects of rock music. Today's pop-rock hits are usually dance tunes—and feature strong and evocative rhythms. In this section, you'll focus on hits of the classic pop period as you play the music of Cat Stevens, Elvis Presley, and the Beach Boys.

Morning Has Broken

"Morning Has Broken" is a traditional hymn that captured the attention of Cat Stevens. In 1972, his hit recording of this beautiful tune stayed on the pop charts for eleven weeks, peaking at position six.

This arrangement of "Morning Has Broken" features arpeggios in the left hand—and will sound best with a smooth and connected (legato) quality throughout. First practice the chords.

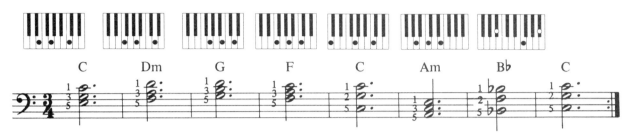

The dynamic markings in "Morning Has Broken" will help bring out the personality in your performance. The marking *p-mf* indicates that you play the first verse softly and the second verse medium-loud. For this song, you may wish to lift and depress your sustain pedal at the beginning of each measure. This is the pedal of the far right of a standard piano. If you are using an electric piano or synthesizer, you may evenutually want to add a sustain pedal to your instrument (if you don't already have one).

Morning Has Broken

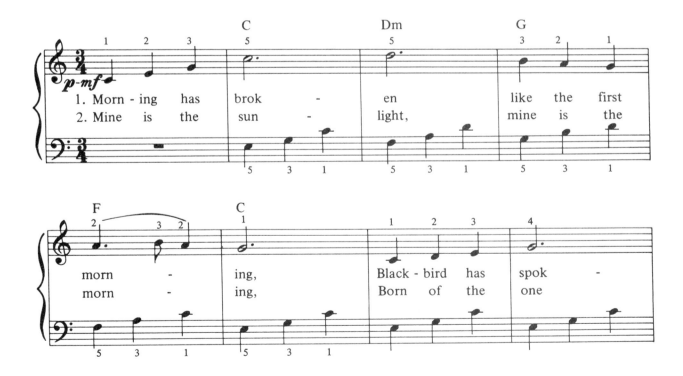

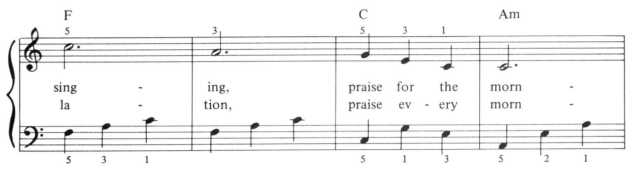

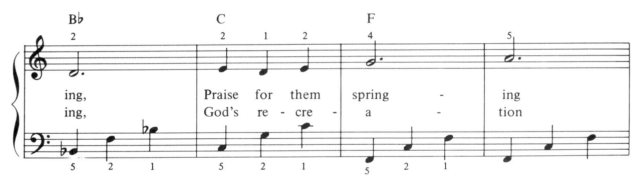

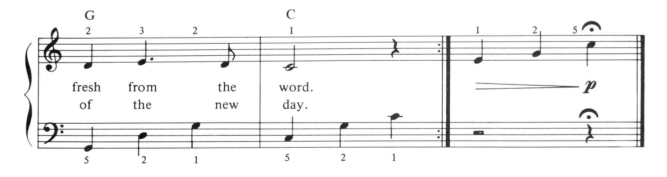

Sloop John B.

Originally a West Indian folk song, the "Sloop John B." became a favorite of the Beach Boys in 1966. Their recording of this classic tune stayed on the chart for ten weeks, topping at the third position. The steady rhythm and lilting melody of their recording made it a natural winner on the pop charts. Practice this chord exercise—which includes the F, Bb, C7, C9, and Bbm chords.

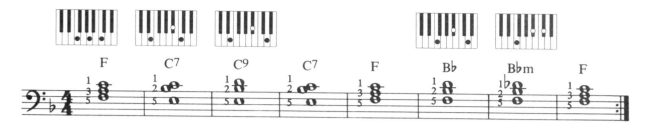

Once you are familiar with the melody of "Sloop John B.," play this tune at a slow to moderate tempo with both hands.

Sloop John B.

We came on the sloop *John* B., My grand-fa - ther and

me, A - round Nas-sau town we did roam,

Drink - ing all night, Got in - to a fight,

I feel so break up, I want to go home.

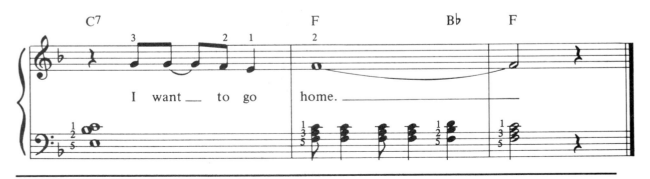

Aura Lee (Love Me Tender)

"Aura Lee" (composed by George R. Poulton) has long been considered one of America's most popular love melodies—and it enjoyed a smash revival in 1956 when Elvis Presley recorded it as "Love Me Tender." This chart-busting hit was the title song for Elvis's first movie—and stayed in the number one position on the charts for five weeks. This popular tune made it back on the charts when Richard Chamberlain recorded it in 1962—and Percy Sledge, in 1967.

Elvis's hit tune makes a terrific slow pop-rock piano solo. Before you play the arrangement, practice this exercise to get familiar with the chord sequence that provides the harmony in the left-hand part. Several chords are used in this exercise—including G, Am, D, D7, G+, C, and Cm. Note that the *G+ chord* is a new chord form called *G augmented.* Some of the chord inversions in this exercise require a full octave stretch of the left hand. Because two of the chords in this exercise are quite high on the bass staff, they are written in treble clef. This is a challenging chord exercise that may require a little extra practice—but the results in "Aura Lee" are well worth it.

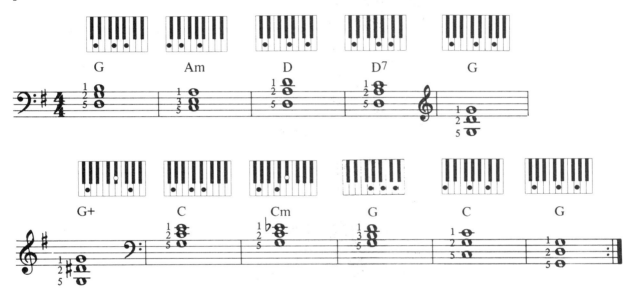

Once you are familiar with the chord exercise, practice the left-hand part of the arrangement, which features an interesting arpeggio pattern. Note the two basic arpeggio fingerings: **5-2-1-2** and **5-1-2-1**. Practice the left-hand part slowly and evenly until you can play each pattern smoothly in tempo. Refer back to the chord exercise for the keyboard position of any chords you can't read.

Now add the melody with the right hand and play this beautiful love song with both hands together.

Aura Lee (Love Me Tender)

Ragtime and Jazz

Most historians agree that jazz is a direct descendant of ragtime and the blues. Like the blues, ragtime emerged from the traditional Black-American folk music of the nineteenth century. Ragtime's inventors are thought to be travelling minstrels who combined elements of Euro-American folk dance and fiddle music with syncopated African rhythms to create a new distinctive musical genre. Ragtime music was characterized by a syncopated melody played with a steady, march-like harmony part.

Ragtime created a sensation wherever it was played—and, in its day, was considered by some to be overstimulating, and even sinful. However, ragtime devotees couldn't seem to get enough of this hot new musical style (which fostered some controversial dance crazes). Ragtime has enjoyed lasting fame in the music of Scott Joplin—who was the first ragtime composer to put his music on paper. In this section, you'll play Joplin's most famous piece, "The Entertainer," and then move on to some tunes from the jazz era.

Jazz first became popular in the New Orleans area at the turn of the century. This early jazz is often termed *New Orleans jazz.* Like the blues, once jazz spread to other urban centers around the country, it took on new forms. Dixieland and Harlem style jazz added some sophistication to the basic sound—and explored the potential of different instruments in the jazz band.

Like its predecessor ragtime, jazz music explored suggestive new rhythms that raised some eyebrows among the conservative set (and inspired many new dance crazes among the more adventurous). In the 1920s, jazz entered the mainstream of popular song and made its debut on the Broadway stage. Since jazz is largely an instrumental form, musicians found that many older songs could be "jazzed up" to enjoy successful revivals. If a song got played enough by jazz musicians, it became known as a *jazz standard.*

Through the years, jazz has claimed many popular songs, folk tunes, and blues songs for its own. These jazz standards include traditional songs like "A-Tisket A-Tasket" and "Frankie and Johnny," as well as commercial hits like "Tea for Two" and "Alexander's Ragtime Band." In fact, most of the songs written by jazz-influenced composers such as Irving Berlin, George Gershwin, and Jerome Kern were reinterpreted by jazz musicians as standard pieces in their performance repertoire.

In this section, you'll play a mainstay in the jazz repertoire—"A-Tisket A-Tasket." After you are familiar with this song, you may feel the urge to explore different variations of melody, harmony, and rhythm—an advanced jazz technique called *improvisation.*

The Entertainer

In 1973, Marvin Hamlisch adapted compositions of Scott Joplin to create the score for the Academy Award–winning film *The Sting.* Joplin's ragtime classic "The Entertainer" served as the theme song for the movie—and became a gold-record hit for Hamlisch in 1974. The popular movie soundtrack and hit single created a renewed public interest in ragtime music—and made Scott Joplin's name a household word for the 1970s and beyond.

Practice this chord exercise with your left hand.

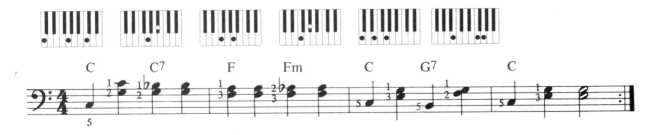

Now play "The Entertainer" at a moderately slow tempo.

The Entertainer

A-Tisket A-Tasket

Ella Fitzgerald is perhaps the greatest jazz singer of all time. After winning the Harlem Amateur Hour in 1934, she created a popular sensation with her jazzy rendition of "A-Tisket A-Tasket."

The secret to a successful jazz performance is a rhythmic technique called *syncopation*. Syncopated rhythms focus stress on beats which are not normally stressed in other forms of music. For example, classical, rock, and pop compositions in $\frac{4}{4}$ time feature stress on the first and third beats of each measure, as in the first lines of "A-Tisket A-Tasket," shown below.

A jazz composition in $\frac{4}{4}$ time often features syncopated notes and words just before or after the stressed beats of the music—on the *offbeats* or *upbeats* of the rhythm. Ella Fitzgerald used this type of phrasing to achieve a swingy feel in this number, as illustrated in the arrangement below. Before you play "A-Tisket A-Tasket," practice this chord exercise, which features the Cmaj7, C6, Dm7, and G7 chords.

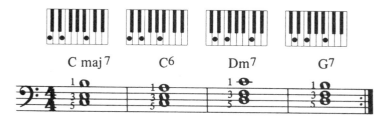

Once you are familiar with the chord exercise, practice the right-hand part of "A-Tisket A-Tasket." Then play the song using both hands.

A-Tisket A-Tasket

dropped it, ___ I | dropped it, ___ And | on the way I | dropped it; ___ A

lit-tle girl - y | picked it up ___ and | put it in her | bas - ket.

Classical

Technically speaking, classical music is any serious music composed between 1750 and 1820. This term is also commonly applied to music of a serious nature composed in any period—from the late Renaissance to the present. Throughout the centuries, classical composers have concentrated much attention on the development of musical structure and form in their work. With the invention of new musical instruments and playing techniques, each generation of classical composers has worked to explore the limits of solo, ensemble, and orchestral performance.

Some classical pieces achieved lasting world fame because of their association with important events in everyday life. Graduations, weddings, funerals, and religious holidays are often commemorated with the performance of particular classical works that have become an integral part of these important ceremonies. In this section, you will learn to play Mendelssohn's famous "Wedding March," as well as Elgar's "Pomp and Circumstance" (the high point of every school graduation ceremony).

Wedding March

Felix Mendelssohn's "Wedding March" from the opera *A Midsummer Night's Dream* was composed in 1844. This stately piece was performed at the wedding of Princess Victoria of England and Prince Frederick William of Prussia in 1858. Until this day, Mendelssohn's "Wedding March" is a favorite choice for wedding processions. It is often performed with Richard Wagner's "Wedding March (Bridal Chorus)" from the opera *Lohengrin*—as occurred at the royal wedding of 1858.

Like any march in $\frac{2}{4}$ time, this piece should be played with a steady and confident beat—with a little extra stress on notes that occur on the first beat of each measure. The dotted-note rhythms add power and importance to this world-famous wedding march.

Wedding March
(from *A Midsummer Night's Dream*)

1. Guid - ed by us, thrice hap - py pair,
2. Home joys di - vine, home joys so pure,

En - ter the door - way, 'Tis love that in - vites.
Love ev - er faith - ful, And love ev - er sure.

All that is brave, all that is fair,
All that is brave, all that is fair,

Love now tri - um - phant for - ev - er u - nites.
Love now tri - um - phant for - ev - er u - nites.

Pomp and Circumstance

"Pomp and Circumstance" (also known as "The Graduation Song") was written by Edward Elgar for the coronation of King Edward VII in 1901. The title is taken from William Shakespeare's *Othello,* Act III, Scene 3. This stately classical piece is best known as the processional music at graduation ceremonies throughout the world. Adrian Kimberly even put it on the pop charts with her recording in 1961.

Practice this chord exercise.

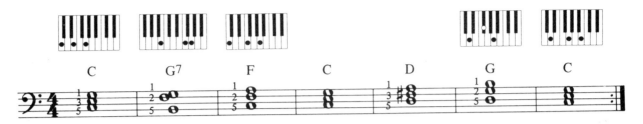

As with "The Wedding March," this piece should be played at a slow and steady tempo—with some extra stress added to notes occurring on the first and third beats of each measure.

Pomp and Circumstance

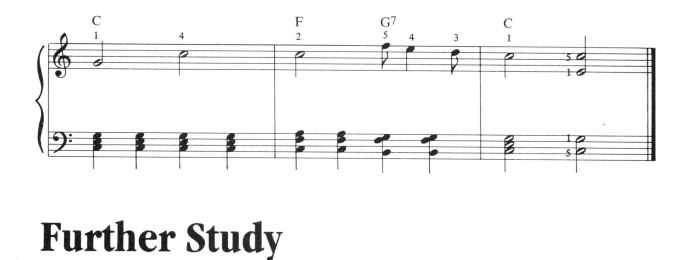

Further Study

Congratulations! You have completed a comprehensive course in piano that will provide a broad foundation for your continued development of your piano skills and personal playing style. The "Table of Notes" and "Table of Chords" that follow will provide you with the key to hours of further study. Use these to explore reading and playing the chords and melody of your favorite songs, as well as ones that are unfamiliar to you. You'll find hours of enjoyment reading through sheet music and song collections as you strengthen these important reading skills.

You may also wish to pursue an in-depth study of chord forms and structure, as is provided in any good music theory textbook. This further study is also advisable for those who wish to compose or arrange music. A basic understanding of the more advanced theoretical aspects of written music can only serve to enhance your piano playing abilities. (Naturally, a well-recommended piano teacher would also greatly enhance your self-study program.) However, at this point, you have all the facts you need to continue your development as a knowledgable and competent pianist—and the music store and music library will provide you with many new doorways to a lifetime of playing enjoyment.

Table of Notes

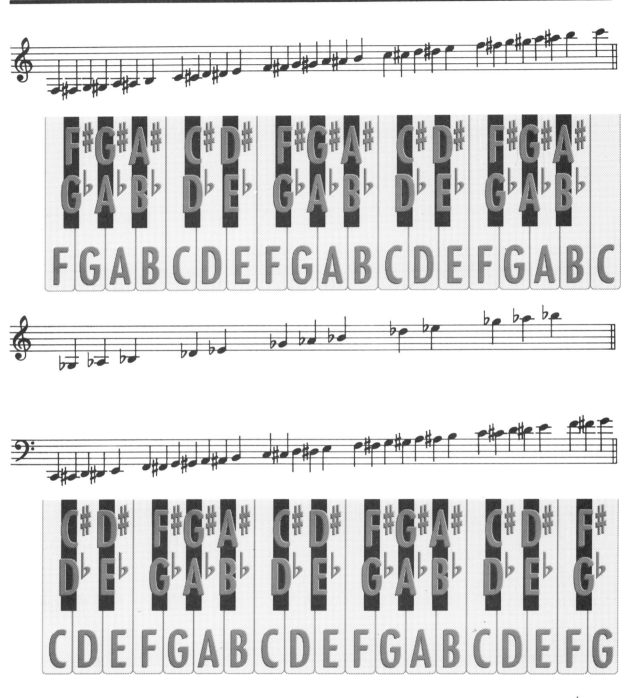

You Can Play Piano

Table of Chords

This table includes basic chords in root position. Remember, you can rearrange the individual tones of each chord to form chord inversions.

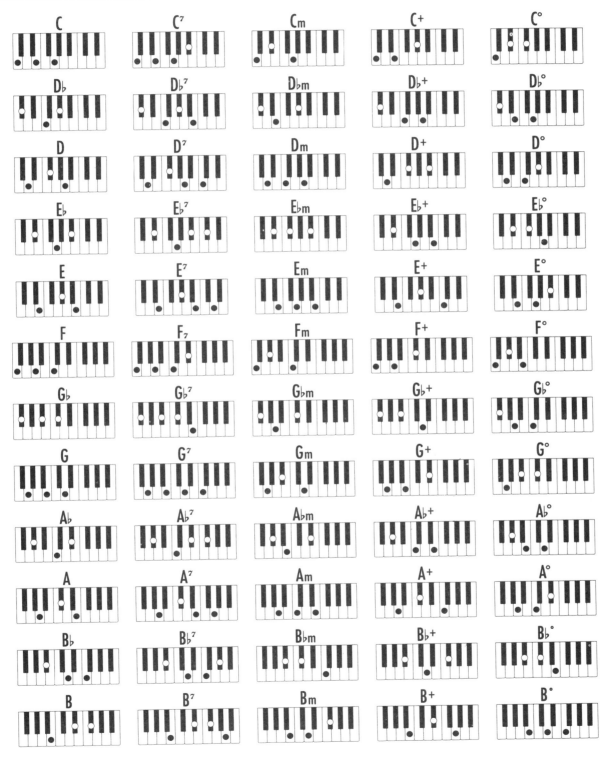

Compact Disc Track Listing